Joanne M Smith /2019

Praise for
THE PRICE AND PROFIT PLAYBOOK

"In today's world of constant tension between the value a firm creates and the price they ultimately receive, it takes a committed, holistic and strategic perspective to truly optimize profitability effectively across any business. This book is the ultimate insider's playbook of how one of the world's great organizations was able to achieve tremendous success through Pricing & Profit Management Excellence in a relatively short period of time. A must-read for leaders of pricing, marketing, or really any type of commercial business function."

—Todd Freeman, Former Group Manager of
Marketing Effectiveness, DuPont

"I have first-hand experience using the approaches discussed in this book. They effectively drove significant profit improvement for my businesses. If you are looking to transform your pricing, I recommend this read."

—Keith Smith, Former DuPont Vice President and
General Manager, Engineering Plastics

"I have been a longtime fan of Joanne Smith, who's rapid rise at DuPont from chemical engineer to pricing guru provided the road map for successful implementation for setting and getting prices—driving superior and immediate results on company profitability. Setting and getting prices requires innovation and

commitment to process. Her "playbook" will lead managers to effect transformative change while delivering prosperity within organizations."

> —Mark R. Leffler, Vice President Development, Connection Chemical LP and Assistant Professor of Management, McGowan School of Business, King's College

"A strategic guide on building an organization that can get the price right. The book delivers a painstakingly detailed process that is tried and tested to deliver superior results."

> —Meena Panchapakesan, Former DuPont Marketing Effectiveness Manager

"Driving large-scale change in a multi-national company is difficult under the best circumstances. Driving large-scale change in pricing, the domain of all and none, is nearly impossible. Joanne's experience, as described in her book, is thought-provoking and contains insights with practical business application."

> —Richard Hayes, Principal, Deloitte Consulting LLP

"This is an insightful, pragmatic view of pricing—with all its daunting complexities--from the practitioner's perspective. Joanne helps the reader to understand the business obstacles she faced, and then the strategies, approaches, and tools she employed to tackle them."

> —Lisa Thompson, Principal, Deloitte Consulting LLP

The PRICING and PROFIT PLAYBOOK

A Practical and Strategic Guide to Generating Superior Profits Based on DuPont's Success

JOANNE M. SMITH
Former Pricing Leader for DuPont

Bradley Publishing

Bradley Publishing: 122 Hartefeld Drive, Avondale, Pennsylvania 19311

First Edition. Printed in the United States.
ISBN 978-0-9897238-0-0
Library of Congress Control Number: 201391334

Editor: Barbara McNichol Editorial
Proofreader: Jeanne Marie Blystone
Cover and Design: Kerrie Lian under contract with
MacGraphics Services

To my husband Keith, my best friend
and greatest supporter,
and to my children, Brad and Jamie,
who are priceless.

Contents

Introduction: The Building Blocks of Pricing Success

Which is the only component of the Four Ps of marketing—product, promotion, place, and price—that most directly brings in a Fifth P—profits?

You got it. Price. I have heard executives say, "I know I am wasting half of my marketing communication budget, I just do not know which half." Well, I never heard them say that about price probably because they had little to no pricing budget.

While companies invest their resources in "product, promotion, and place," they often underestimate the value of investing in smart *pricing* performance. That's a costly mistake! Missed opportunities in pricing commonly lead to 5-10% revenue loss, which for many businesses could translate into lost earning potential in the range of 50-100%.

That's the equivalent of a $1 billion revenue business with $200 million in pre-tax earnings missing out on up to $100 million in revenue and $100 million in earnings.

Now, I'm not advocating less investment in product, promotion, and place at the expense of pricing because clearly these three Ps are part of the foundation for creating or capturing value. However, I *am* suggesting that pricing is equally important and that ultimately, it's best to manage the other three Ps with price and profitability in mind.

I believe five essential elements are needed to deliver superior performance through pricing. In this "playbook"—based on the lessons I learned as former head of DuPont's global pricing organization—you'll discover how you can apply these elements to improve your company's pricing.

DuPont's Playing Field

First, let me introduce DuPont, a bio-science and chemical company founded in Wilmington, Delaware, in 1802. This highly diverse company consists of businesses ranging from industrial, automotive, packaging, agricultural, and nutritional to those involved in safety, electronics, and protective apparel. While DuPont is predominately known as a specialty products company, pockets of commodity products are included in its portfolio.

In 2004, it was nearly a $30 billion revenue company—but it could have been noticeably higher. For by that time, DuPont's average price had been steadily declining and the company had been experiencing eroding variable margins for more than a decade. Realistically, the company was leaving billions of untapped earnings potential on the table. Why? Because of poor pricing strategy and execution or, more accurately, the lack of urgency and attention to pricing.

This eroding margin proved to be the burning platform that propelled DuPont to focus on price.

In that year, I joined the newly emerging team to improve the company's pricing performance. As the leader for improving pricing across nearly 60 diverse businesses, I learned many things (sometimes the hard way) that have proven to be critical to achieving outstanding pricing and profit results.

Bravely and frequently, DuPont took non-traditional approaches and charted new ground. By 2010, it had become a leader among specialty chemical companies in reversing the pricing decline and achieving significant pricing gains. To realize that level of profits, my group and I sought pricing knowledge from marketing and pricing consultant firms, professional societies, books, courses, and articles, as well as numerous other business-to-business companies. I can confidently report that a tremendous amount of valuable expertise is available.

However, the path to gain this knowledge wasn't smooth. Many of the sources I consulted focused only on certain sub-elements of pricing, with some advice being more theoretical than practical. Among this sea of choices, I was challenged to find what I needed or create my own path. I wished I could turn to a holistic, systemic "playbook" that covered change management and strategy through price-setting methods, people and competency, processes, systems, and execution. More important, I wanted this playbook to help me deliver big results fast and consistently.

Well, after learning from external sources, applying that to diverse businesses within DuPont, and developing new approaches, I've created *the* playbook I wish I'd had when I started this journey. Throughout this playbook, I provide you with the practical tips and guidance I've found essential. It's my sincere goal to help you successfully improve *your* company's pricing performance.

The Structure of This Playbook

There are many parallels between what it takes to create a company with superior pricing and what it takes to create a professional sports team with winning seasons. So, at times, I have used sports analogies to help illustrate the key concepts needed for successful pricing.

Think of any successful sports team and you will recognize the large combination of factors that contribute to its success—from the extensive efforts to find the right coaching staff and players, to the strategies and tactics that go into the playbooks and training, to the rituals and equipment. And don't forget the ongoing, extensive research needed to determine the opponents' strengths and weaknesses.

The same combination of factors is critical for building a winning pricing company.

This playbook is divided into five sections that present the five elements, or "plays," essential for transforming a weak or mediocre pricing performance in the business-to-business arena. With a focus on practical, quick-hit ways to improve both financial results and competency, this book only touches on pricing theory/techniques that support these ideas. Don't expect deep price-setting theory here; numerous excellent books cover this aspect in depth.

The five sections, or plays in this playbook, include:

1. **The Right Corporate Team & The Right Culture:** This first section covers the roles, team makeup and skills needed from your corporate level pricing leadership and experts. It also focuses on the critical aspects of your company's culture and the leadership behaviors essential to support strong pricing.

2. **The Right Business Team:** The second section focuses on the roles, team makeup, and skills needed from your business-level pricing experts as well as the broader marketing and sales organizations within the company.

3. **The Right Pricing:** This section explains how to set the right price. It covers transactional, value, and strategic pricing, with a focus on practical, quick-hit ideas.

4. **The Right Execution:** The fourth section details how to execute a price increase or (counter-intuitively) a price decrease to maximize your success.

5. **The Right Systems:** This last section focuses on the key processes and information systems that enable smart, effective pricing day after day, month after month.

Common Pricing Fumbles

The plays listed above address head on these common pricing "fumbles" that B2B companies experience:

- *Failed price increases*

- *Little adherence to pricing guidance*

- *Limited respect for the pricing organization personnel*

- *Few or haphazard price increases over the previous 5-10 years*

- *Sales department with wide pricing authority*

- *Industry with decreasing prices year after year*

- *Pricing that's typically used as a key vehicle to gain market share (or "buy" share, as I like to say)*

- *No clear ownership for pricing in the organization; it's a side job of marketing or sales*

- *Little or no pricing expertise to guide pricing decisions, processes, and tools*

- *A broadly held belief that you can't control price; it just happens to you*

- *The practice of allowing volume and/or revenue growth to dominate marketing and sales behaviors*

- *Leadership that places little priority or urgency on pricing and has no personal skin in that game*

- *Little understanding or practice of transactional pricing, value pricing, and strategic pricing.*

TRANSACTIONAL, VALUE, AND STRATEGIC PRICING

If you don't know the difference between these three, your business probably doesn't practice them.

- **Transactional pricing** refers to your pricing execution for each transaction. It is tightly linked with your sales execution and leaking value from your list price.

- **Value pricing** refers to pricing for your specific value to a given customer/market segment and is deeply integral to your marketing strategy.

- **Strategic pricing** refers to your ability to influence industry pricing in a positive direction and is heavily integrated with your business strategy.

My DuPont Experience

Let me set the stage for what you're about to learn in the chapters that follow.

For more than six years, I led a pricing transformation for the DuPont Company. It started at a time when our company had no pricing group, no pricing analysts, and no pricing managers. Essentially, DuPont had no pricing *competency*. None. And not surprisingly, our pricing performance was quite weak. For example, many of our businesses had not successfully increased prices in years despite many attempts to do so, while other businesses had not even attempted it even when increases were justified.

For over a dozen years (or as long as I could get my hands on data), the company's variable profit margins were continually eroding over 10 percentage points—a hard pill to swallow for a company that prides itself on its premium products. But in that era, volume and revenue growth ruled, while any focus on pricing took a back seat (like the last row of the bus).

Fortunately, in 2004, DuPont's CEO Chad Holiday recognized the value of smart pricing. In fact, he made it *the* top priority of our newly created Corporate Marketing and Sales organization. Chad showed a bold commitment by appointing one of his senior group vice presidents, Diane Gulyas, to be chief marketing officer (CMO), reporting directly to him. Diane, along with Director Mahesh Mansukhani, began the task of forming the new organization.

At this time, I was in Europe providing internal business and marketing consulting to our DuPont European businesses. The chance to play an important role in the start-up of DuPont's Corporate Marketing and Sales organization—and focus on pricing—was right up my alley. Without delay, I moved back to the States to help with the creation of the pricing organization. After a year or so, I shifted into the role of Global Marketing and Pricing Director, reporting to our CMO.

What was our initial pricing goal and my number one objective? To stop our margin erosion and build pricing competency across DuPont.

PRICING DEFINED

Pricing is the process of setting the value you should receive for your offerings based on marketplace and competitive dynamics, customer needs, quality of the offering, costs, and your pricing strategy.

The pricing process also includes negotiating prices, administering prices, and monitoring/managing pricing results.

As I define pricing in this playbook, it goes beyond this traditional definition. It includes challenging and refining the business and marketing strategies through product and asset choices to create the best company and industry pricing and profit dynamics.

Despite our CEO's strong support, our pricing journey was a tough one. At the time, DuPont had roughly 60 business units grouped into 16 strategic business organizations. Each strategic business organization had autonomy for running its businesses. Rarely did Corporate impose specific activity on the businesses.

To get started, we shifted 15 internal business, marketing, and general process consultants into pricing consultants—albeit untrained, unskilled pricing consultants. Thus, there we were in our new corporate group—one that could only influence businesses but had no decision-making rights—with 15 business consultants who had limited or *no* pricing experience. Let the games begin!

DuPont Scorecard

I'm delighted to say, our group experienced enormous success almost from the beginning. By the end of our first year (2005), we had achieved over $300 million in pre-tax profits (which paid for the investment in pricing)—a revenue increase of over 1% from 2004. In subsequent years, we achieved results of roughly $500 million a year through pricing projects and influenced further pricing successes to total benefits of nearly $1 billion a year. In fact, we delivered seven straight years of pricing increases, which included 22 straight quarters of "quarter over quarter" pricing increases followed by only two "down" quarters during the 2009 recession, after which quarterly increases resumed. (See Figure 1.) For Six Sigma fans, that represented a statistically significant change in pricing performance. It gave our group, and the company, a reason to feel extremely proud.

During the severe recession that began in 2008, most businesses experienced a 20% or more decline in industry demand. Customer pressure to reduce price soared. In fact, customers threatened to shift to new suppliers if we didn't drop our prices. So using newly developed approaches, we selectively dropped our prices, carefully and thoughtfully, to minimize the necessary price decline. (During this recession, most chemical companies had to drop price to remain competitive.) Then, as the economy picked up in late 2009 and early 2010, we carefully brought prices back up to pre-recession pricing and beyond.

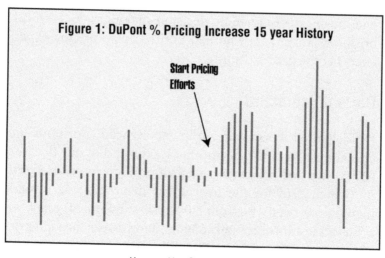

Figure 1: DuPont % Pricing Increase 15 year History

Year-over-Year Quarterly Results

At the end of the day, we made progress on our variable margin erosion and recaptured over half the margin we had been losing for more than a decade. To be fair, I acknowledge that the cost of raw materials was going up fast during the mid-2000s, thus playing into our pricing success (though severely challenging our ability to regain margin). It gave us a fair and credible justification for passing these costs along to our customer base.

But keep in mind, we (like the rest of the industry) had also gone through several periods of high raw material prices over the preceding decade, before we added pricing resources, and we had been unsuccessful in passing along the raw material increases to our customers. In fact, the company decreased pricing over the previous decade despite the favorable market dynamics for raising price. Clearly, having favorable market conditions without the pricing resources and skills was not enough for pricing success.

An advantage of leading the pricing efforts across a large diverse company was the opportunity to quickly see trends and thus accelerate our learning curve. As we began our pricing efforts, I talked with many business leaders in DuPont who told me they'd tried to raise their price several times over the past few years with little or no success. As a result, they were highly skeptical that we could help them turn that around. Additionally, they were greatly concerned they'd lose market share.

Next Challenge Faced Head On

Appropriate opportunities to raise price over those previous years had most certainly arisen, so clearly, price *setting* was not our only skill gap. Price *execution* was also part of the problem. I gradually came to realize that even more factors had influence. These included culture, strategy, people, processes, and systems, not to mention the kitchen sink. (Just joking. The kitchen sink was fine.)

Fortunately, I love a good challenge and my own sweet spot embraces facilitating change. Despite my strong business management and marketing background, however, I was—like the rest of my team—"lite" on deep pricing experience.

A chemical engineer by training, I was drawn to this field by my love for problem solving. After years of running chemical plants, I shifted into business and marketing management, in which I've spent the bulk of my career. My problem-solving skills (and the fun) evolved as I incorporated culture change and systems thinking into my approach to achieve both greater and longer-lasting results.

I can trace my passion for problem solving back to third grade and Mrs. Till's class. It quickly became clear to me I could rapidly see patterns my classmates did not. This trait goes even deeper because I look for quick ways to solve problems and implement practical, efficient solutions. For me, that involves reaching out extensively to any and all sources of knowledge I can find, then uniquely combining the best of them to arrive at the bottom line—namely, sustainable financial results.

After two years of working on DuPont's pricing, I was discussing with a colleague if we should keep working on pricing or shift our focus to broader marketing competency. My colleague questioned the value of continuing with pricing because he suspected we were 80% finished with possible improvements in that area. Fortunately, we didn't walk away from the issue. We'd actually only scratched the surface, and the more we learned, the more we realized how far we were from true pricing excellence.

The challenges grew; the need for integrating business and marketing strategy into our pricing work became even clearer; and the rewards garnered by our changes increased. As this book explains, we came out winners.

The Coach's Timeout – Quick Hit Tips

As a pricing coach, my guidance is grounded in the following 10 recommendations for pricing success. Based on experience and research, I've come to believe these recommendations are *necessary*. We'll explore each of these in more detail throughout the book.

1. Smart pricing takes extraordinary courage and risk taking, broad cultural change, and strong leadership as well as skilled people that go well beyond the pricing resources. The top business, marketing, and sales leaders in the company must be proactive partners in leading price initiatives. Often that means behaviors from the CEO down through the sales organization must change.

2. In addition to your business pricing resources who manage the day-to-day pricing, having a

small group of centralized pricing leaders and change agents is essential. This group has a dual purpose: (a) performing periodic advanced pricing analysis and pricing projects in the company, and (b) spearheading the development of company-wide pricing skills, capability, processes, systems, and culture.

3. The centralized pricing group should be led by a high-level, credible, empowered leader/change agent capable of influencing the beliefs and behaviors of the CEO and senior leadership throughout the full business, marketing, and sales organizations.

4. Centralized experts should be a blend of top talent with both experienced business leaders and young MBAs or young professionals/engineers with business leadership aspirations. These pricing roles can and should be valuable training roles for future business and marketing leaders.

5. Your central pricing resources and your business day-to-day pricing resources must have the respect and support of the business, marketing, and sales organizations. This respect comes from delivering results and demonstrating an understanding of business and marketing acumen as well as market dynamics. It also comes from being a true partner with the marketing and sales organizations.

6. Using external pricing firms and industry groups, initially as well as periodically, is an efficient and essential way to accelerate your pricing improvements as well as critical to build the initial skills within your pricing organization.

7.   *Transactional, value,* and *strategic* pricing are all essential elements to address, yet often one or more of these is overlooked. Start your pricing efforts with *transactional* pricing; it takes the least skill while helping you obtain fast financial gains. These gains are essential to building the credibility you'll need for broad support.

8.   Effective pricing (especially *value* and *strategic*) often changes or informs your business and marketing strategies. Thus you need a handful of strong, experienced business/marketing leaders in your central pricing group, and pricing should be integral to your marketing efforts and organization. (I believe a lack of appreciation for the strategic skills required is a key reason pricing initiatives fall short in some organizations.)

9.   The company must invest in good systems that drive good pricing processes to enable fast, smart decisions to be made and executed.

10. Measuring results and *making those results visible* are both critical strategies for gaining credibility. Set "stretch" goals and go for them full out!

Are you ready? Let's check out the elements of a good game plan.

PLAY 1:
THE RIGHT CORPORATE TEAM & THE RIGHT CULTURE

Any team owner who wants his or her team to win game after game, season after season, needs to begin by recruiting the right head coach and players as well as setting the right environment for success. It's the same when you want your company to win the pricing game and consistently achieve superior profits.

You need a "head" coaching team (which may include player-coaches—players who also coach). Ideally, these people form a central or leveraged group to lead the company initiative, bring the deep advanced pricing knowledge, drive the needed culture changes, and make the improvement last. Leveraged refers to resources that will work across different business units or industries rather than be dedicated to one specific business or industry. This head coaching team will guide and supplement each business unit's pricing leader (or coordinator) and its pricing players who do the blocking and tackling of daily pricing.

Think of it this way: Would the owner of a professional football team hire independent coaches for the offensive team, the defensive team, and then the special teams reporting directly, with full autonomy, to the general manager? No, because they recognize the absolute necessity of having these teams work together under the same overall direction set by the head coach. Yet, like the pricing leaders needed in each business, these coordinators do have significant authority and accountability to lead improvement in their sub-teams, provided their actions align with the overall team's direction. And just as businesses have unique dynamics and needs, so do the offensive, defensive, and special teams. Yet superior success comes only when they honor and balance both the differences in these sub-teams and the advantages that come with a holistic team approach.

This Play will take a clear look at what it means to have:

- *the right people with the right skills as your top pricing leaders and*

- *the right corporate direction and culture.*

Chapter 1:
The Right Corporate Pricing Group

Every good team needs a savvy coach, or in this case, a coaching group. If you want to go from pricing for *mediocre* profits to pricing for *superior* profits, you need to play in the major leagues with professional coaches and a highly competent starting lineup.

The role of any great coach is to teach, guide, and motivate. Effective coaches walk the fine line between providing support and enforcing discipline. Your central group needs to both drive a step change in performance *and* instill confidence and unity in the players, fans, and owners.

The three main goals of the pricing leadership group are to:

1. Drive better pricing results across the company by periodically leading advanced pricing analyses and projects within the company or each business entity within the company.

2. Improve pricing skills across the company's marketing, sales, and pricing groups through training courses and other developmental efforts.

3. Build a culture that fosters a passion and urgency for price and profit growth by:
   a. communicating a compelling business case;
   b. influencing company objectives or reward systems; and
   c. influencing the behaviors of the company's top leaders down through the sales force.

Why have a small central group with strong talent? For these four main reasons: *leverage, acceleration, credibility,* and *impact.* Let's see how each of these plays out.

By working on the toughest business pricing problems and encountering various issues across diverse businesses, the central group members gain deep knowledge at an accelerated rate. This allows them to work faster and smarter in subsequent business projects. As they leverage their knowledge and accelerate projects for greater impact, they enhance their credibility as experts. As their credibility increases, the businesses begin vying for their help. (Note that when I refer to businesses, I mean not only various businesses within a company, such as those under the DuPont umbrella, but divisions or departments within one business.)

The central group is like a football team that extensively practices advanced plays and frequently plays against highly diverse teams. Compare this to a business pricing group, which might be closer to a football team that predominately practices the basics and consistently plays against the same team. Clearly, the central team with its more advanced training will be better equipped to deliver results.

A central group is well positioned to form networks between businesses or divisions as well as note trends across the company. For example, these experts may see that certain businesses are faced with the same pricing problems or similar macroeconomic issues. This overview allows the team to develop solutions that can be leveraged and communicated across the businesses to accelerate their financial impact.

For example, between 2005 and 2012, many businesses faced similar issues. These included oil prices skyrocketing along with prices of basic materials and the global recession that followed. In DuPont, the pricing group provided corporate solutions to benefit the businesses such as 1) freight and fuel surcharge best practices, 2) broad-based corporate price increase communications from our CEO to our customer base, and 3) proactive guidance for pricing in a downturn.

Because of the high-value work of the central group—from advanced pricing projects to company culture change—the company can justify recruiting high-level talent. These people are able to gain respect and credibility quickly. In turn, that credibility allows them to effectively motivate others, influence the leadership, and foster desired professional behaviors in the businesses.

Lastly, a central group can be tasked with a large, eye-catching financial target—essentially the sum of the desired business units' pricing improvements. That large financial target, along with the credibility of the group, significantly improves the odds of gaining the attention and active support of the CEO. This support is critical to achieving many of the changes the central group must tackle because these adjustments may be company-wide. They will likely affect company objectives and priorities, information systems, reward and recognition programs, and organizational structures and roles.

Your first thought may be: "In my company, each of our businesses are unique and thus they need the freedom to fully run their own pricing in a way that best meets their individual needs." If so, I urge you to think again. While I agree that many aspects of pricing must be individualized for each business, the numerous benefits of a corporate team (as noted above) still outweigh this argument. The central group is the way to go, but those leaders must respect, honor, and meet the individual needs of the unique businesses to be successful.

Okay, you still may not think having a central group is feasible in your company. Such a structure may go against your culture, or perhaps only one business unit sees the value in improving pricing. Or, you may think it wouldn't work because your company is a smaller single business.

Never fear; the game isn't over before it begins. You're just playing with a handicap, like a team with an injured key player. In this type of situation, the rest of the team will need to man up; take up the slack and cover this gap. Like a handicapped team, you can incorporate as many of these ideas as possible into your approach. Rather than a central group, you might have a few people within your business who take on the roles and responsibilities described for the central group. Let's see what those entail.

Choosing Your Pricing Leader

Job one is to select your head coach, the global pricing VP or director. This leader must have demonstrated the ability to drive significant change and garner credibility or possess the ability to quickly gain it across the company. Although having someone with extensive pricing experience is ideal, a seasoned business/marketing leader with the skills of a strong change agent could do the job. In fact, business acumen and strategic marketing skills are more valuable than deep pricing expertise over the long haul. You may start a little slower but you'll finish stronger.

Like a coach, the prospective pricing head's leadership skills must include visionary and direction-setting abilities, innovation, and strategic thinking. In addition, this leader must have a proven aptitude to influence others and work effectively across all functions and levels. I suggest having this leader report to the chief marketing and sales officer, a group president, or in smaller companies, the CEO.

Consider this: If your company does not yet have a marketing leader, which may involve skepticism about the value of investing in marketing, then positioning pricing as the first step in your marketing improvement journey may serve you well. As far as marketing goes, pricing is the fastest way to achieve meaningful profits and thus a great way to build marketing credibility. It's also a natural way to back into the other elements of marketing. For example, if you're doing value pricing, the customer information you gather to understand your value can easily lead you to refining your products or offerings, improving your market communications, or even segmenting and serving your customers based on their values and needs.

THE PRICING LEADER'S PRIMARY RESPONSIBILITIES

What is the pricing leader's primary role? Setting the vision and direction for change, then effectively leading the execution of this vision. This leader has to address the seven key actions for any successful change:

1. Obtaining leadership buy-in and appropriate behaviors

2. Creating a compelling vision

3. Making the business case for change

4. Deploying resources for success

5. Adjusting systems and structures to support the new vision

6. Monitoring and rewarding performance

7. Taking actions to ensure the change lasts

In marketing terms, the leader must both *create* demand for help from the businesses and *fulfill* that demand. That means it's not enough for the central pricing group to have experts, project methodologies, best pricing practices, and tools available. The leader, or VP/director, must generate the desire—plus the *urgency*—in the business to ask for the group's help and value that help when it comes. (You'll learn ways to do that successfully later in this chapter.)

Beyond stirring up interest, the pricing leader might also lead or provide guidance to the business pricing projects. However, this level of help is likely to be a secondary priority for the leader, especially as the pricing group matures and others can step in. You could think of it as the coach determining the play—even doubling as quarterback to start the play—then handing the ball off to other team members to complete the execution.

In my first few years as pricing director for DuPont, I spent as much as 60% of my time leading or coaching pricing projects with the businesses. As my own team grew in expertise, I shifted into spending 60-70% of my time leading and driving the broader aspects of the vision. That included adjusting systems and structure and making change last. The all-important step of making change last clearly involved transferring pricing skills, confidence, urgency, and passion throughout the business, marketing, and sales areas across DuPont.

Building Your Pricing Team

The pricing leader or coach is the one to build the pricing team, meaning the extended coaching staff and coach-players. For DuPont, my team functioned in a consulting capacity—with a twist. We were accountable to the CM+SO (chief marketing and sales officer) and the CEO to ensure that specific pricing targets were achieved across the company, but we needed to do this through influence. The businesses weren't obligated to follow our guidance or invite us into their business to lead or help with their projects. As mentioned earlier, we walked that thin line between support and discipline, as great coaches must do. We conducted the tough, candid discussions needed to develop the courage in others so they would act on aggressive pricing moves that inherently risk volume.

Given the complex science of transactional, value, and strategic pricing, companies have an ongoing need for pricing experts to support everyday pricing activities within business units. However, businesses often consume their pricing resources with the basic day-to-day "blocking and tackling" of administering and monitoring pricing. They don't always have the time (nor is it practical for them) to develop the deep skills they'd need only occasionally.

Thus, leveraging the expertise of the central pricing group to periodically conduct "end-run" advanced projects in the various businesses is both an efficient and effective way to improve pricing results. Team members can dedicate time to conduct deep market/customer, competitor, cost, and performance analyses. Equally important, they bring credibility and influence to establish business leadership buy-in for actions.

In DuPont, most businesses wanted an advanced pricing project once or twice a year. In our first year or so, our projects focused on less advanced methods, such as *transactional* pricing. As the businesses developed the skills to do the transactional work themselves, our projects shifted to the more difficult aspects of pricing (*value* and *strategic* pricing) as well as major overhauls in processes and systems.

High Skill Level is Required

As on any team, having a high skill level for your central team members is key. Yet this is an area in which companies often fumble. You need to do more than hire price analysts. The team must blend pricing managers who have deep business, marketing, and leadership experience with pricing analysts who have the potential to be future marketing leaders.

The number of resources will depend on the size and complexity of your company. For an organization with a few billion in revenue, I suggest starting with two or three mid-level managers and twice that number of young, upcoming future leaders for a total of six to nine. Typically, resources work in teams of one manager to two junior analysts. In DuPont, a company with roughly $30 billion in revenue, we started with a global team of about 15 located in Wilmington, Delaware. We supplemented them with external consultants in the early years. Eventually, we provided a few additional resources in each of the regions.

When hiring prospective *pricing managers,* look for skills such as deep business/marketing experience and strong leadership and problem-solving skills. In addition, they must have the ability to interact with business leaders in ways that engender confidence and influence behavior. Having deep pricing experience certainly comes in handy, but it can be learned. Thus if you have a few pricing managers and can't find individuals with both marketing and pricing expertise, consider blending marketing experts with pricing experts.

These pricing managers will become the heart of your pricing expertise, thus you need to do whatever you can to ensure they remain in these roles for at least three to five years. Like a championship sports team, your team can't afford high turnover. Even the unexpected loss of one key player makes a big difference. (You may remember what happened when the Indianapolis Colts lost Peyton Manning to a neck injury in 2011. Hello losing season and bye-bye Super Bowl aspirations!)

Pricing managers typically lead project teams staffed with two junior central resources and one or two appropriate business resources. They're also idea partners for the global pricing leader. While it's recommended they gain deep expertise in all forms of pricing, you can also provide each with a specific pricing area to "own" for which they develop the content (i.e., transactional, value, and strategic pricing and process/systems). They might split their time 70-80% leading pricing projects, 10-20% developing the next-generation pricing methodologies, and 10-20% assisting the global pricing leader in the broad change initiatives.

Before forming our corporate marketing and sales group in DuPont, we had an internal centralized consulting group that focused on business strategy, marketing strategy, financial consulting, and general process consulting. Roughly half of these consultants were repurposed as our initial pricing managers. Some were excellent fits, while those without strong marketing backgrounds and/or strong analytical skills were eventually placed in other roles throughout DuPont.

Over the first few years, we strengthened the team by hiring a few experienced marketing managers as well as an experienced competitive intelligence consultant. Competitive intelligence consultants, like football scouts, have deep expertise in research techniques to gather knowledge about competitors. Typically, they focus on gathering background such as a competitor's strategy, strengths, weaknesses, asset plans, cost, and capacity—all of which is critical knowledge needed for pricing.

The key to our team's early success (when our pricing skills were still weak) was aligning with the business consulting firm of Deloitte, especially their marketing and pricing departments (see www.deloitte.com). This alliance got us off the ground and quickly delivered results. In no time, our internal resources developed the skills to independently lead projects.

A word of advice: When hiring or drafting your *central pricing analysts,* target young people with leadership potential and/or recent MBAs. Look for those with strong problem-solving and analytical skills. At DuPont, these resources typically held the roles for one to three years, with the MBAs staying closer to one year.

During that time (and depending on their skills), we gave them greater and greater responsibility, from initially being analysts on projects to leading small projects themselves. The exposure they got across the company was invaluable in their development and networking. The work itself accelerated the learning of business and marketing skills. At the end of their assignments, the call for these individuals to join business teams was quite high. They moved into roles such as marketing managers, product-line managers, or strategic pricing leaders.

We had excellent experience with young top-talent engineers who aspired to move into business roles. The company supported them in earning their MBAs in the evening, and they were energized by the role and its implications for their career development.

At DuPont, we also had some highly satisfactory but admittedly mixed experience with recent MBAs. Having worked with numerous recent MBA hires from a variety of top schools, I've concluded that MBA programs are weak on teaching deep, practical pricing. But the background they provide does include analytical and problem-solving skills, which allows their grads to add value quickly. In addition, the marketing background provides an excellent foundation to rapidly learn strong pricing skills.

Equally important, these MBA graduates gained an understanding of the company and what it takes to be successful, while building strong networks of their own. Why the mixed results? At times, some believed that doing analysis was "beneath" them, that they should be *running* the project (or the company!). My advice: If you're hiring recent MBAs, keep assignments on the short side. Also give them as much responsibility as they're capable of handling, and provide them with opportunities to meet and network with the corporate business leaders. That sets up a win-win situation.

Upgrading a Team Already in Place

You may come from a company that already has a central pricing group. That can be both a blessing and a liability.

On one hand, your company has access to more pricing knowledge—a blessing. On the other, if you don't have the fundamental critical elements (e.g., high-level reporting, top talent, credibility in the company), it's a liability. You'll need to address this liability to become more effective.

In football, we see coaches change and players traded and drafted. Sometimes creating change can be painful, but making a few bold moves may be your best bet. Bring in a high-powered leader who reports to a senior company leader, along with one or two top-talent mid-level managers (from internal or external hires). Over the next year, gradually transition the rest of the group to the top talent and future leaders you aspire to have—your all-star players.

Are you still questioning whether this team seems a little too overpowered or overeducated for your company? Are you thinking you can get by predominately with pricing *analysts*? If so, I urge you to reconsider. These game-changing plays that educated and strong marketing talent bring are needed to turn mediocre performance into great performance—and higher profits.

Read Chapters 6 and 7 in Play 3 on value and strategic pricing; they will shed further light on the necessity for this skill level.

Build Your Fan Base—or Raise the Skills of the Commercial Teams

If you want home-field advantage, you absolutely must have the support of your cheerleaders, band, and fans, which come in the form of your marketing and sales organizations.

Who is accountable for building this fan base? The central group. It must instill passion, urgency, confidence, discipline, and skills throughout the company with respect to marketing and sales. Only when it does this successfully will the company reap the benefits.

Success also depends on the marketing and sales organizations supporting pricing recommendations and *executing* them with confidence and skill. In addition, you need this extended group to independently recognize *and act on* pricing opportunities they see in their daily work.

The first step is to get the attention of the marketing and sales organizations. Do they understand the value of excellent pricing skills? Do they realize the critical role they should be playing in this area? If the answer to both of these questions is yes, then do they think they need to improve their skills? Chances are they'd be surprised at how much they don't know.

When I started in pricing, I would have rated my own pricing skills as fairly good. But after six years of focusing heavily on this area, I look back and realize my pricing skills were mediocre. You know the saying, "The more you know that you don't know, the more you know"? Well, this applies broadly when it comes to pricing across the B2B landscape.

How do you get the marketing and sales folks in the game and let them experience the possibilities firsthand? The good news: This should, in part, happen naturally as the central group runs successful pricing projects in the businesses. It's essential, though, that the business, marketing, and sales leaders be directly involved during projects. They need to be either key people on the *project* team or part of the *steering* team responsible for executing the recommendations.

HOW TO INSPIRE YOUR MARKETING AND SALES FOLKS

Bringing in pricing projects is an excellent initial opportunity to teach, guide, and build the confidence and courage of those in the marketing and sales areas. There's nothing like firsthand in-the-game experience and financial success—high scores—to open their eyes to the power of pricing.

But conducting projects alone is insufficient to make the internal changes you need. Following are a number of other successful ways to both win the hearts and minds of the teams and build their skills. The list is long because it takes many different ways over several years to build a strong "fan" support.

- **Hold semi-annual half-day Pricing Summit conferences.** *Make them open to all business, marketing, and sales leadership. Showcase successful business leaders by having them share their pricing success stories and their key learnings. Add interesting speakers, such as a successful pricing or marketing leader from a different company, an economist, or a sourcing VP, to provide a variety of perspectives. Focus these summits around your current reality. For example, in November 2008, during the early days of the big recession, I held such an event called "Pricing in a Downturn Summit." The topic appealed to those in our commercial organizations who* *were clamoring for guidance. Turnout was high, and participants responded with extremely positive feedback.*

- **Form a Pricing Champions Network and request that a marketing VP or director of each business join it.** *This network would provide informal direction to the central pricing group as well as a forum to share the businesses' pricing environment and price learnings. The group members will learn from each other and appreciate the opportunity to influence the central group. Members shift from being observers and judges to being partners.*

- **Provide price training courses geared to marketing/ product-line management roles.** *For example, offer two-day courses on "Advanced Pricing," open to commercial leaders. (Note: The Monitor Group conducts such courses. The consulting firm was recently acquired by Deloitte: www.deloitte.com.)*

- **Provide price-negotiation training geared to sales and dealing with price pressure.** *Various outside groups offer this specialized training. In DuPont, we used "The Bay Group International" consulting and training firm. (Note: This group has recently been acquired by Corporate Visions: http://corporatevisions.com.)*

- **Write and distribute monthly or quarterly newsletters.** *This is a way to share pricing articles, success stories, and pricing tips and guidance. The Professional Pricing Society is an excellent source of pricing articles, as is the consulting firm of Holden Advisors: www.holdenadvisors.com.*

- **Distribute timely communications with background and guidance during changing pricing times.** *These might include market downturns, high fuel costs, or market upswings. For example, early in 2008 at DuPont, we were* *sensing the market would weaken in the second half of the year. Our guidance encouraged businesses planning 2008 price increases to shift them into the first half of the year when the pricing dynamics were likely to be much more favorable than the second half of the year. In retrospect, this advice was right on point and noticeably increased our pricing gains in 2008.*

- *Provide tools and best practices, and list your central group's pricing services on a user-friendly website.*

- **Present webinars.** *Hold occasional short webinars, open to all business, marketing, and sales organizations, focused on skill building or immediate pricing issues. For example, in DuPont we held webinars on sales compensation, fuel surcharges, and sales policies.*

- **Measure and drive pricing maturity.** *Pricing maturity describes how skilled a business is in pricing relative to world-class pricing. Assess businesses on their pricing maturity, make them aware of "good pricing," and keep these maturity metrics updated and visible. (Chapter 3 addresses maturity models in more detail.)*

- **Influence senior leaders to set expectations for their marketing and sales teams.** *I found it useful to hold monthly calls with both DuPont's Economist Office and Sourcing leadership to get a pulse on what they were experiencing in the environment. This, along with sensing and studying market demand, helped foresee coming changes in the pricing environment with sufficient time to prepare senior leaders and the company.*

Whenever possible, our communications—seminars, webinars, newsletters, etc.—were geared toward the largest concerns affecting the businesses' pricing decisions at the moment (or even better, in the near future). They raised early awareness of the issues and provided practical advice, best practices, or tools. However, to do this effectively, members of the central group had to continually monitor the marketing dynamics, stay close to the business issues, and keep closely connected with external pricing and marketing experts. Then they had to quickly develop solutions or guidance as needed.

SOME HELPFUL EXTERNAL PRICING AND MARKETING EXPERTS*

- Deloitte (marketing and pricing consulting – www.deloitte.com)

- Monitor Group (marketing events by invitation and training – now owned by Deloitte – www.deloitte.com)

- Holden Group (monthly pricing newsletter – www.holdenadvisors.com)

- Professional Pricing Society (newsletters, conferences, and training – www.pricingsociety.com)

- Bay Group International (price pressure negotiation training)

Based on first-hand experience. Additional good sources are available.

Win an Invitation to the Bowl Game—or Get the Businesses to Ask for Your Help

If your company is like DuPont, your businesses can choose to use your central group's help or not. But even if Corporate requires them to use you, unless you have the business's willing support, you're unlikely to get the priority, resources, and results you want. Thus it's important to not only develop what you have to offer but also *create the demand* for these offerings.

You need to be invited in at their request. Fortunately, your team's expertise in building the skills of the commercial teams will naturally create demand. In addition, positioning from your CEO and senior leadership helps immensely, so work with your CEO to publically and proactively advocate for pricing effectiveness.

Hold a Post-Game Evaluation—or Craft a Project Review

As you do projects for a business, be sure to finish with a project review for the business president. In our initial years in DuPont, we included our CM&SO in the review. The following advantages of doing a project review have proven to be substantial:

- *For the business, reviews reinforced the importance of executing recommendations to deliver results, as well as the power of price in delivering profits.*

- *For the chief marketing and sales officer, the review provided firsthand knowledge of a success story. That story could be included in company-wide communications to senior leaders and the broader marketing and sales organizations. It also gave them a natural opening to encourage positive pricing behaviors.*

- *For the joint business/central group project team, reviews provided exposure to leadership and brought recognition for their hard work.*

Wow Your Owners — or Get Support from the CEO

In football, you "wow the owners" by winning game after game. In business, the only surefire way to gain and keep the CEO's support is to deliver results in the form of revenue and earnings!

So as you begin the pricing game, set a goal that's big and tough enough to be important to your CEO. As mentioned earlier, I have seen the large majority of businesses easily achieve 5-10% revenue uplift over the course of a few years—with many that far exceeded this amount. In fact, of the hundreds of pricing projects we executed in DuPont, many included several pricing projects in the same business (i.e., one on transactional price, another on strategic price, a repeat project one year later under different market conditions, etc.). All of them delivered more than a 1% revenue uplift from price improvements, with the majority delivering 3-5% per project and some delivering as much as 40%!

A pricing increase per year (in dollars) that's equivalent to 1-3% revenue uplift over and above your recent historical price increase performance is a good, conservative ballpark number to shoot for (in non-recessionary times). Remember, this increase comes from pricing. And depending on your variable margin and operating profit margin, it can produce roughly a 10-30% improvement in profits. (For example, this holds true for a 40% variable margin and 10% pre-tax earnings margin business. If margins are lower, the pricing impact on profits will be even higher. Conversely, if your margins are higher, the pricing impact on profits will be lower.)

If you're diligently following this playbook, you should exceed this goal. So if you are a $2 billion revenue business, target at least an additional $20 million/year of earnings; $20 million/year in year one, an additional $20 million/year in year two, etc.

Once you've set your goal, be sure to keep the metrics visible to people throughout the organization. I suggest tracking two things at the company level: 1) the benefits from the projects led by the pricing group and 2) the bottom-line company price change year-over-year (measured on a quarterly basis). Of course, the benefits won't start showing up in the financial sheets for about six months. However, by the end of the first year, you should see a definite positive return on the investments.

Kick Off the Season

If you're starting out with no pricing group as we did in Du-Pont, don't wait until everything is perfect. Begin as soon as you have the fundamentals in place.

The minimum fundamentals include a *global pricing leader* and at least a few central pricing resources in place. Then, if budgets allow, bring in an outside consulting firm to partner initially with your resources so your internal team members can learn on the job. Focus on transactional projects at first because they take the fewest skills (data collection and analytics, for the most part) but offer a quick way to find price leakage and plug it. Deloitte is an example of an external consulting firm that excels in this area and can jumpstart your pricing improvement and knowledge transfer.

Ultimately, your central group needs to be able to lead advanced marketing/pricing projects. These include performing customer segmentations through designing differential offerings with differential price points. They will also need to assess multi-year market dynamics and design business model changes that will lead to higher current and future pricing and profit realization.

Be confident and believe that your team players—like pro athletes—can and will grow into these skills. As they do, your pricing leader can be diligently working on influencing the corporate culture so it enables and supports good pricing.

Chapter 2:
The Right Culture

Throughout the previous chapter, I mentioned a number of ways to build a culture that properly enables pricing success. This chapter provides additional thoughts on the subject in more depth.

When you think of the top priorities in your company relative to top-line growth, what comes to mind? Share growth, innovation, volume growth, variable/profit margin growth, pricing growth? Okay, but if pricing and/or variable margin trends are not on your priority list, you need to think again.

It's imperative to understand and embrace the *value* of pricing as your largest lever for profitability. You have an up-hill battle if any of the following statements or attitudes is *pervasive* in your corporate culture:

- *Essentially the only real way to increase our profitability is through innovation and share gain.*

- *The best way to meet our strategic objectives is through share growth in emerging regions.*

- *The market sets the price; we don't.*

- *Pricing is the role of Sales.*

- *Pricing is the role of Finance.*

While share and volume growth, as well as innovation, are clearly critical to strong business performance, they're insufficient. In fact, single-sided thinking like this can actually hurt profit growth.

Remember, no other business lever is as powerful as price for improving your profitability. Not volume gains, not variable cost improvements, and not fixed-cost improvements. Pricing improvement can generate *two to four* times more earnings than equivalent percent improvements in volume for a business with 25-50% variable margin. The improvement factor is greater for lower variable margin businesses and slightly lower for higher margin businesses.

Innovation (or at least market driven innovation) as a profitability lever is great in that it brings new value offerings. However, without pricing skills, you may not capture your full fair share of the compensation. Furthermore, new innovative products are likely to represent 2-5% of your product base. So even optimally pricing these new products won't impact it enough to offset mediocre pricing in the 95-98% of existing products.

With returns on pricing so great, why do so many companies seem to under-invest and undervalue pricing relative to their other initiatives? The biggest reason may be the underlying belief that the *market* sets the price, thus price is largely out of an individual company's control. That myth needs to be quashed.

As discussed in the strategic pricing chapter, most companies (excluding extremely small players) can and do have an impact on market pricing. Their actions, whether intentional or inadvertent, do affect price. I have seen this time and time again. When price is not strategically managed, the effect is often an inadvertent negative pressure on market price. However, when managed well, it frequently creates a positive impact.

The myth that "pricing is the role of the sales department" is another death trap. Don't get me wrong; Sales has a critical role to play in pricing, but it's never the lead role. The number one job of the sales team is to build customer relations, then parlay these relationships into business growth.

Sales people tend to believe that increasing price only makes their challenge more difficult. They often don't have the opportunity to see the big picture—the multi-year strategic view and the overall impact of their individual actions on the market. Price strategy through price setting is a key role of business and marketing management; they must own it and use it as one of their key strategic levers. Likewise, sales leadership must own the execution of price to the targets and policies set by the business.

The belief that a company's finance function should *lead* pricing is a limiting proposition. While the finance people are likely to be helpful with analysis and maintaining adherence to policies (with transactional pricing), it's highly unlikely they have the skills, knowledge, or credibility to drive the more important aspects of pricing optimization (i.e., value-based and strategic pricing).

FIRST THREE STEPS TOWARD PRICING EXCELLENCE

1. Convince the company's leaders of the value of pricing excellence and the extreme business risk of overlooking this lever.

2. Persuade the top leaders to accept their personal roles and accountability in driving pricing excellence. They cannot be bystanders.

3. Commit leaders to investing in pricing competency with company resources, systems, and training.

At a corporate level, CEOs are wise to set company- or business-specific expectations and objectives regarding pricing (or margin) improvement—perhaps including pricing (or better yet margin enhancement) in his/her annual company critical operation tasks (COTs). These margin objectives can then cascade down to the specific business level.

Setting variable margin improvement objectives (price minus variable cost) is often more effective then setting price objectives, especially in times when raw material prices may be changing significantly, as it is a truer measure of whether you are extracting more value or less value. While a 5% price increase may sound impressive, it is not if your raw material prices have increased 20%. Conversely, if raw material prices are falling and you are able to hold prices, thus increasing your variable margin, this is a positive outcome. But be cautioned, measuring only variable margin is insufficient. Businesses should also consider secondary measures to assure their actions result in maximizing the total variable contribution dollars. Thus they will also need to be evaluating price/volume and or product mix effects.

In DuPont, our chief marketing and sales officer—as a member of the CEO's executive leadership team—effectively drove these corporate objective changes for the company.

Additionally, the CEO must routinely ask about price/margin performance and improvement plans just as he or she would for volume/share growth. As mentioned earlier, if the CEO is serious about changing the company's performance, it's important to invest in high-level pricing change agents. After that, the next step is to set specific dollar goals for the corporate pricing team and measure the progress.

If you recall, a general rule of thumb is this: If you're new at pricing transformation, a reasonable goal would be to achieve the equivalent of 1-3% revenue uplift (~10% pre-tax profit uplift) within the first year or two.

Business presidents and leaders need to have even more skin in the game than corporate leadership. Pricing can be difficult, unpleasant, and even risky. Your marketing and sales people are probably used to being rewarded and valued for their growth capabilities. You're asking them to potentially risk their growth/volume efforts to increase price—something they may not feel quite skilled in or comfortable doing. They will likely project more downside risk then upside reward and, quite naturally, shy away from this less known and risky effort.

Time and again, I've seen a top leader have to make the tough call to raise prices, overriding the fears of others in the organization. Just like a head coach might make the risky decision to go for a long-shot touchdown versus a reasonably sure-bet field goal. In addition to making their expectations and urgency clear, the best leaders couple these decisions with four additional actions:

1. They articulate that loss of volume is quite possible, and they will shoulder this risk. They clarify that the company will be walking closer to the "cliff edge" in finding its true and fair price point; only after it loses a little volume will everyone know the edge is near.

2. They make sure decision rights, responsibilities, and accountabilities are clear across the functions and regions. They also ensure sufficient resources are devoted to the effort. (This is not the time to expect that price-increase efforts are to be accomplished in the evening after folks have completed their normal workload.)

3. They proactively build confidence in the organization. Confidence is based on knowing they can effectively implement this increase, that it's the right thing to do for the business's health,

and that it's fair (albeit unpleasant) for the customer base.

4. Lastly, they listen with empathy to people's concerns, but they hold firm to their position and remain consistent with their message.

As a leader, if you take this route and negotiations result in lost sales above your tolerance level, you must re-evaluate. However, in the hundreds of price-increase efforts I've witnessed, more than 95% led to no volume loss—much to the great surprise of those in the whole organization. And for the few cases in which some volume loss occurred, roughly half of these customers came back within a matter of months.

Of course, you never know the results until you try, and thus you and all involved must have courage and conviction.

In DuPont, the culture change was visible and significant, moving from a volume growth mindset to a price and profitable growth mindset. The confidence of the commercial teams followed, accompanied by significant change. The most visible and impactful actions taken by our corporate leadership included:

- *forming the corporate marketing and sales group,*

- *funding the corporate pricing experts,*

- *seeding the effort with funds to utilize external consulting experts,*

- *setting pricing and margin improvement targets as one of the few key annual corporate objectives,*

- *supporting pricing system upgrades, and*

- *frequently including pricing and margin improvements in on-going formal and informal communications.*

Corporate leadership also took a visible interest in the businesses' progress toward improved pricing and profitability results. In addition to the results, that included understanding the pricing resources and skills the business was building.

That's the next play in your playbook to consider.

PLAY 2:
THE RIGHT BUSINESS TEAM

Winning game after game takes more than just having the right managers and head coach in place. The assistant coaches, the players, the cheerleaders, the band, and the fans all contribute to a successful season. This holds true if your company wants to consistently achieve superior profits from its pricing: All involved must know their roles and have the skills needed to perform well.

In each business, you need a leader—an offensive coordinator—to encourage and drive change. You need the pricing players in each business unit to do the blocking and tackling of daily pricing. And if you want home-field advantage, you absolutely must have the support of your cheerleaders, band, and fans in the form of your marketing and sales organizations.

The next two chapters focus on what you need to know to have the right people, the right skills, and the right objectives for these business groups:

- *Business pricing resources*

- *Marketing and sales organizations*

Chapter 3:
The Right Business Unit
Pricing Group

Businesses make pricing decisions every day. For example, they set list prices, announce price increases, negotiate customer-specific prices, approve price exceptions, set pricing term policies, and approve exceptions to these policies. Ensuring the best decisions requires your business to have the right resources and people with the skills and authority to guide both decision making and improvements in your processes and systems.

This "play" provides guidance on structuring your business-specific pricing roles and responsibilities.

Building the pricing resources of a business can take very different forms. It all depends on your price and profit objectives, the complexity and nature of your product line, your business dynamics, and your enabling systems (or lack of systems). But one thing is for sure: Pricing is not just the role of the pricing manager and analysts. The business or commercial leadership and the people in sales must also play a large role. (This is discussed in more detail in the next chapter.)

From my experience, it's important to consider the following questions when designing your business pricing resources:

- *What improvement objectives and tasks do you want to achieve?*

- *What roles and responsibilities are needed to achieve your objectives?*

- *Who in the organization has which decision rights relative to pricing as well as the other price-related aspects of marketing (product, positioning, place)?*

- *What is the appropriate reporting structure considering career paths?*

- *What is the complexity of your product line and customer base?*

Also, consider where you are on a pricing maturity continuum. Are you a novice at pricing or closer to being world class? What do you aspire to be in one to three years? The higher your aspirations and the larger the gap between those and your current state, the more you'll need strong resources dedicated to pricing.

Pricing and Profit Objectives

Use the following list as an idea generator to help you set your aspirations and objectives relative to your current state. Which of these potential objectives would you like to achieve? Also think about the timeframe for achieving these objectives—perhaps three years.

- *Drive organization buy-in and culture change. Work with the leadership to promote the need and motivation for change that supports price and profit success.*

- *Create the vision and multi-year game plan to achieve your price-related objectives.*

- *Drive pricing competency. Lead the appropriate skill development across the full commercial team (i.e., leadership, marketing, sales, pricing, and product-line management).*

- *Provide thought leadership to central pricing group members to help them set their direction and objectives.*

- *Drive strategic, multi-year pricing strategies and be a price leader in your industry, making the business strategy changes needed to foster higher future profits.*

- *Develop market and/or customer segmentation*, differential offerings*, and differential pricing structures* to maximize growth and profit. (See *Pricing Terms defined in the sidebar.)*

- *Transform your businesses into "value merchants": Quantify value, develop value propositions and value-in-use pricing,* then communicate and sell value. (The term "value merchants" was coined in the book **Value Merchants** by Anderson, Kumar, and Narus.)*

- *Create or refine your pricing processes, from price setting through price administration* and deal management.*

- *Upgrade your data quality and systems to manage your pricing processes, adhere to price targets* and policies, and manage profitability performance.*

- *Develop value-selling tools* to enhance the execution of value-in-use pricing.**

- *Set or recommend list prices by market segment and/or customer needs-based segments.*

- *Approve exceptions from list or floor price targets.**

- *Manage transactional pricing from administering price at a granular level, tracking and analyzing profitability and value leakage* as well as monitoring and enforcing price and policy adherence.*

*PRICING TERMS

Market segmentation: Clustering or grouping different market segments based on factors such as similar needs, profitability, or strategic intent. Usually done with the intent to manage each segment differently.

Customer segmentation: Clustering or grouping different customers based on factors such as similar buying behaviors or needs. Usually done with the intent to serve each segment differently.

Differential offerings: Creation of different offerings to serve the unique needs of different customer groups, generally offered at different prices. For example, they might be labeled Gold, Silver, and Bronze offerings.

Differential pricing structure: Different prices for different market/customer segments. Typically, the offering (product plus services and terms) will differ with the price.

Value-in-use pricing: Pricing the offering (product and services) based on the value to the customer and relative to the customer's alternative choices. As an example, if your offering provides the customer with an advantage of $2/unit over competitive offerings, then a value-in-use price might be $1/unit above competition, presuming you split the benefits with your customer.

Price administration: The process of administering price, from recording new price lists to recording negotiated prices and terms, then accurately billing the customer.

Price target: The price at which you wish to sell your products—an internal number used to guide the sales organization. This can be equivalent to the list price or the price you publically post; however, if most of your prices are negotiated below list price, then your target price is likely to be below list price.

Value-selling tools: Any tools that help your sales force sell the value of your offering, e.g., value calculators, value-based communication tools.

List price: The price you publically quote or post to the industry. It is typically the highest price you might achieve, but often you will negotiate discounts off of this price list based on things such as the volume, the shipping container, or services.

Floor price target: This price is the lowest price that the sales force can drop or negotiate the price down to without requiring special management approval.

Value leakage: This refers to anytime you are not fully and fairly compensated for the value you provide the customer. Examples include underpricing, offering too favorable payment terms, and not billing or collecting on agreed-to charges such as late payment fees or surcharges for less than truckload quantities.

The objectives at the top of this list are the more strategic ones and require a higher level of leadership skills. Those in the middle are geared to value pricing and require strong marketing experience. Those low on the list tend to be more tactical than the others and require analytical skills or information-systems capability.

If your business is a mix of specialty and commodity products, and you aspire to be very strong in pricing, you may want to aspire to the full list.

Roles and Responsibilities

Most business leaders are likely to select a list of objectives that require these three distinct roles:

- *Strategic pricing champion or leader*

- *Pricing manager(s)*

- *Pricing analyst(s)*

In football terms, these roles might equate to a defensive coordinator, a defensive captain, and the defensive players. Not all of these roles need to be full time. Some of them will likely be a part of the marketing VP/director, marketing manager, and/or a product-line manager position. However, if you decide to include them as part of other positions, ensure that those people 1) have a clear priority for their pricing objectives, 2) have sufficient time (no less than 35% of their work schedule) to properly perform the work, and 3) have or can develop the proper training/skills. *Advice:* I wouldn't recommend making all three of these roles part-time if you're serious about effecting change.

Let's discuss each of the three.

The Strategic Pricing Champion

The strategic pricing champion, or leader, should be a high-level leader who sits on the business leadership team and, ideally, one who has demonstrated change leadership. Typically, marketing vice presidents/directors take on these pricing objectives as part of their overall role. The primary responsibilities of this function include the following:

- *Lead the business toward world-class pricing.*

- *Drive any needed cultural changes to inspire the organizational urgency.*

- *Establish the priorities necessary for optimizing pricing to maximize profits.*

- *Set the vision and determine the game plan.*

- *Drive the adoption of—or improvement in—pricing strategies, competencies, processes, systems, tools, and incentives.*

- *Act as a thought partner for the centralized group aimed at improving the company's overall pricing and profit results.*

- *Establish the business's pricing resources, including clarity of responsibilities.*

The strategic pricing champion will rely heavily on the central group for support and guidance.

The Pricing Manager

The pricing manager(s) is often someone with strong marketing and/or product-line management experience. The primary responsibilities might be:

- *leading and driving strategic pricing, that is—*
  - *understanding and tracking competitive intelligence on costs, capacity, and strategy;*
  - *monitoring industry sales/capacity and other strategic pricing levers;*
  - *recommending pricing moves and competitive responses;*
  - *driving effective price communications.*

- *driving/co-driving value-in-use pricing, that is—*
  - *facilitating market or customer segmentation;*
  - *encouraging differential offerings with differential pricing per segment;*
  - *developing value quantification;*
  - *developing value-selling tools and value-selling communications.*

- *setting pricing policies and leading process and system improvements.*

- *managing pricing analysts and overseeing their transactional pricing responsibilities.*

Because these responsibilities may be difficult to tackle, they could be split among a few people (provided they each have the time, priority, and skill required). A product manager might be responsible for the strategic pricing elements, and a market/industry manager might have responsibility for the value-based aspects.

The Pricing Analyst

The pricing analyst(s) needs to have strong analytical skills. The primary role covers:

- *deeply analyzing profitability and profitability leakage;*

- *monitoring and enforcing pricing targets and policies;*

- *administrating price (communicating and posting list and target prices into appropriate systems and organizations, assuring customers are billed correctly based on their negotiated customer agreements).*

Basically, the pricing analyst supports the pricing manager in doing whatever analysis is required.

Who Has Decision-Making Rights?

Clarity of decision-making rights across the organization is critical. This statement warrants emphasizing.

The full organization must understand *who* has the authority to make *what* pricing decisions. Not only is this understanding critical for determining the skills needed for the different pricing roles, but it's essential to eliminate gaps or confusion across the business regarding pricing.

Decision rights are likely spread across the business leader, marketing leader, sales leader, product-line manager, sales force, customer service representatives, and pricing resources. A lot of people need to be involved for pricing excellence. Yet with so many people, it's easy for decisions to fall between the cracks or, equally bad, for everyone to make his or her own decisions. Similarly, members of a football team on game day clearly know who will call the offensive plays—the head coach, the offensive coordinator, or the quarterback. This would certainly not be left to chance.

So who should be responsible for having what decision rights? Specifically, ask these questions:

- *Who approves or decides on market, customer, and product segmentation classifications and prioritization, and the different strategy for each segment?*

- *Who approves or decides to implement broad or segment-based price increases (or decreases)?*

- *Who approves or decides on pricing mechanism(s), for example; $/kg, $/kg of active ingredient, $/ft, $/customer classification?*

- *Who approves or decides the specific floor and target prices for your product line and market/customer segments?*

- *Who approves or decides on sales policies per segment (i.e., lead times, payment terms, minimum shipment size, etc.)?*

- *Who approves pricing processes (i.e., bid process, price approval process, price change process, etc.)?*

- *Who approves pricing information systems?*

- *Who decides on the sales channel (i.e., direct, distribution) for products or customers?*

- *Who approves contract length and terms and/or contract versus spot market decisions?*

- *Who approves exceptions to floor or target prices?*

- *Who approves exceptions to sales policies?*

- *Who approves sales compensation incentives?*

These decision rights are often in the hands of the marketing and sales leadership. Marketing should have the primary decision rights in most of these items; sales leadership should own or co-own the last five items. Some of these may be delegated to your business pricing resources, or these resources may support the marketing and sales leadership in executing or monitoring some items.

When DuPont first started its pricing journey, too often many of these decisions were being made by the sales leader or the sales person. Not surprisingly, this led to a wide variance in pricing and discounting. Naturally, the sales force is charged with creating strong customer relationships. Add to this the fact they're often rewarded for share or revenue growth, and it's only natural to see price suffer. So allowing the sales force to have too much pricing authority can be akin to having the coach from the opposing team referee the game.

Furthermore, a sales person—or even a sales leader for a given region—could inadvertently hurt your overall pricing. That person might decide on a price that seems perfectly reasonable for one customer but results in fallout that hurts your overall market credibility and thus your pricing ability.

CASE IN POINT:
PRICING DECISION GONE AWRY

Here's an example of how your business can get hurt if pricing decisions aren't allocated and confined to certain roles.

Let's say you're implementing a broad-based 10% price increase. A large potential customer tells the sales person that your price is too high and must be dropped 12% to gain the business. Due to the large volume at stake, the sales person agrees to the lower price.

This situation could play out several ways, and all of them would hurt your credibility. The salesman has just taught your customers you're not a value seller—that is, you will drop the price if they push back hard. Competitors, having lost the business, believe that your company is dropping price to gain market share. So they might respond by dropping price themselves (or at least not following your lead with a broad-based price increase). They might even let some of your loyal customers know you're offering lower prices elsewhere.

By making that decision solo, the sales person has, in effect, hurt the ability of the whole sales force to effectively raise price.

> Another possible scenario: The customer goes back to the current supplier and allows that supplier to match the sales person's lower price. Under this situation, you not only don't gain the volume but you've lost credibility in the eyes of the customer and competitor. Thus, you've hurt your ability to be a pricing leader.

Reporting Lines and Career Paths

Where should business-dedicated pricing managers or pricing analysts report—within the business or to the central function?

From my experience, either way can be effective. Ideally, they would have dual reporting, both to the marketing leader in the business and to the central group for functional guidance. *Advice:* Go with what works best in your culture, ensures both credibility and partnership with the business leadership, and supports the career development of the individuals.

If your business/commercial leadership views the pricing resource people as outsiders, unknowledgeable about their business, or too internally focused instead of a valuable partner, it will be difficult for these resources to contribute to their fullest. This is the potential risk of having them reside solely in a corporate function.

Also consider the career progression of the individuals. In professional football, each player has an agent looking out for his career. Pricing resources also need a career mentor and a career progression plan. If you plan on hiring pricing professionals, then it's likely their careers can best be managed through the central function. On the other hand, if you opt to use these roles as developmental assignments for future commercial leaders, then their careers may be best managed within the business structure.

It's been my experience that young top talent who aspire to move into commercial roles can gain excellent personal development from being in pricing roles. One reason is that these roles tend to have high exposure to and interaction with business and marketing leaders. Arranged properly, the up-and-comers often join (if not lead) key business or marketing strategy discussions. After all, any effective business or marketing strategy must address profitability—and thus must consider pricing.

PROFESSIONAL PRICING SOCIETY

Developing your dedicated pricing people can be enhanced through their membership in the Professional Pricing Society (PPS) and involvement in its programs and conferences. For information, go to http://pricingsociety.com.

In DuPont, most businesses that were exposed to strategic pricing were quick to ensure that strategic pricing high-level responsibilities were adopted—often embedded in the marketing director role. This went a long way toward the company's success. However, on the other hand, many of our businesses were slow to add either a pricing manager or pricing analyst, thus hindering our pricing successes for a time. Those that did add pricing managers or analysts actually achieved higher financial results and accelerated their competency as well as their processes and systems.

A word of caution: I often see companies opt to have their pricing resource people report through the Finance Department. While you may find some advantages to this approach in the early days of your pricing development, it severely limits your ability to fully optimize price. If you're tackling transactional pricing only and want your pricing resources either to act as the pricing police or to primarily set price on a cost-plus basis, reporting through Finance will work for you. However, as discussed throughout this book, if you want to shift from *mediocre* pricing to *outstanding* pricing, then intertwine pricing with marketing and business strategy.

It's not about spreadsheets and analytics; it's about deep customer and competitor understanding. It's also about adjusting your market mix (four Ps of product, promotion, place, and price) by segment and potentially adjusting your multiyear business strategy. Fostering that change via the Finance Department can be a challenge.

Product Line and Customer Complexity

If your product line is a handful of commodity chemicals sold in bulk to a few hundred customers, your pricing resource needs are quite low. If you're a large player in your industry, though, you may want a pricing manager who's strong in strategic pricing, including:

- *gathering competitive intelligence,*

- *monitoring macroeconomics,*

- *recommending broad-based price increases or decreases depending on the market dynamics, and*

- *acting quickly and decisively to communicate price changes to the customer base.*

On the other hand, if you have thousands of products going to thousands of customers and they're often specialty products, your pricing resource needs increase. You'll likely need both a pricing analyst and a pricing manager.

Your pricing manager would be wise to pay attention to all the skills listed for strategic pricing, but they will focus more on value pricing, including:

- *understanding value-in-use,*

- *facilitating or encouraging customer segmentation and differential offerings at differential price points, and*

- *developing value-selling communications and tools.*

If you continually introduce new products—and especially if you provide custom parts or equipment (i.e., manufactured specifically for one customer and one application)—the complexity increases and so do your resource requirements. You then need to (1) understand your cost per custom part and (2) develop value-in-use quantification at the custom part level. That means understanding the value your customers receive from your offering relative to their alternatives and be able to quantify this value.

Many specialty business leaders falsely believe they need to focus only on value pricing. They don't think they should be doing broad-based price increases based on macroeconomics. Well, at one time you could take this position, but since 2005, the world we live in (and price in) has changed dramatically. The enormous swings in oil and energy prices, coupled with market upswings to recessions, make it imperative for specialty product businesses to be skilled at strategic pricing. This is needed to ensure you maintain a healthy variable margin as well as keep the pricing gap between your valued-added products at a reasonable premium compared with alternative commodity products.

Likewise, many leaders in commodity companies think they do not need to focus on value pricing. Essentially, they are resigned to being a commodity player. However, with the right set of services, commodity product producers have proven time and again that differentiation, and thus pricing premiums, are possible. So I encourage commodity players to also consider value-based marketing and pricing techniques.

The Pricing Maturity Ladder

In setting a vision, creating a compelling business case to in-spire change, and building a multi-year game plan to achieve your vision, it's helpful to know where you are now. To that end, you want to: (1) understand where your company's or business's current pricing capability is today relative to world-class pricing capability, and (2) determine what you aspire to attain.

Many external consulting firms can help with a pricing capability diagnostic, or you can create your own maturity model. As you get started, all you need is a very simple mod-el. But as you get closer to world-class status, you may want a more sophisticated model to guide you. Pricing Solutions Ltd., a consulting firm, has a well-developed and effective five-step Pricing Maturity Model and tool worth exploring. In DuPont, we started with a fairly subjective five-step model from Deloitte consulting. Later, we developed our own high-ly robust and quantifiable model. More about that later.

Most pricing maturity models have a similar four- or five-step foundation. They then differ in the granularity or details of each step and in the measuring process and tools. The fun-damentals of a very simple generic pricing maturity model might look something like the one that follows, but keep in mind not every business should aspire to be excellent or world class in all aspects of pricing. The nature of your business and your market dynamics should guide you to the high gain areas of pricing for you. So do expect differences between:

- *commodity and specialty businesses,*

- *low complexity businesses versus high complexity businesses,*

- *industries with very short product life cycles versus long product life cycles, and/or*

- *industries with few large competitors versus numerous small competitors.*

SIMPLE PRICING MATURITY LADDER

Top Rung: World Class in Pricing

Designated people seamlessly execute all pricing processes (price setting, price negotiation, price administration, price performance management) in a holistic approach that utilizes a single closed-loop information system. They effectively drive all levels of price setting (transactional, value, and strategy), using extensive customer, market, and competitor research to inform their strategy. Product portfolio life-cycle management is an important part of their pricing strategy.

Price setters effectively use market and customer segmentation to design differential offerings and pricing targets to relevant segments, which the sales force then follows. Value selling tools are widely used by the sales force to quantify, communicate, and document value at the customer- or segment-specific level.

Real-time profitability and performance data is available to the pricing and commercial teams in easily understood formats such as graphs.

The company has a passion for pricing and key players understand how it integrates with business, marketing, and supply-chain strategies. Pricing leaders proactively manage prices across a multi-year timeframe, exerting upward pricing pressure on the market/customers through carefully thought-out pricing, business, and marketing plans. In the meantime, the marketing and sales organization has the skills and confidence to achieve the pricing strategy and targets. The sales force sells on value and is fairly compensated for this value based on enhancing profits and ability to sell value.

Fourth Rung: Strategic Approach with Emerging Optimization

Broad-based pricing capability exists throughout the marketing and sales teams. Both value and strategic pricing prevail and segmented approaches are emerging. Proactive price management has become a key business success lever. Highly capable pricing resources optimize price/volume decisions. Highly confident in their pricing capability, marketing and sales people have the ability to effectively deal with disruptive competitors. Disparate information systems (e.g., a pricing authorization system and price analytics) emerge to facilitate portions of the pricing processes. Market, customer, and competitor research and knowledge gathering are emerging. Market communications are being more frequently used to support higher value perception *and* higher prices.

Third Rung: Established Disciplined Pricing

At this stage, pricing resources and processes have been fairly well determined. Proactive price management, goals, and metrics emerge as people throughout the company now understand the importance of pricing. Value pricing concepts start to become apparent, and quality data is now reasonably available. The marketing and sales organization is developing confidence in its ability to effect upward pressure on pricing. Also occurring are initial steps to rationalize low volume and profitability products.

Second Rung: Emerging Basic Processes and Analytics

Pricing processes and analytics are beginning to take shape. The focus is mainly on transactional pricing and the enforcing of pricing targets. Although pricing capability is limited, portions of the organization are beginning to embrace pricing as a key lever for profitability.

Bottom Rung: Ineffective Processes, Reactive Behaviors Rule

Few, if any, formal pricing initiatives, resources, or processes exist. Pricing may be regarded as a disadvantage; decisions are ad hoc and crisis-driven with a one-off approach (i.e., each decision is taken independently). Signs are not yet apparent that the organization understands the value of pricing, so it isn't actively working to improve its price position. Volume, share, and revenue growth remain the dominate drivers for the sales force.

DuPont's Experience

DuPont was no different than most companies when it came to developing pricing. We started off with the majority of our businesses in the bottom two rungs, eventually shifting into the third rung, with some businesses edging toward the fourth rung. As we improved and moved into the third rung, we developed a much more sophisticated pricing maturity model under the leadership of Todd Freeman. Todd utilized a highly interactive approach with business teams to assess their pricing maturity, but more important, to teach them the possibilities and garner the teams' alignment on their next areas to improve for high-gain benefits.

It's important to note that with the highly diverse businesses and markets in DuPont, we did not expect, nor recommend, that every business achieve the same level of pricing maturity. As we approached the top two levels, we worked closely with the businesses to understand their specific business dynamics well enough to assess which elements would have high payback for that business. Then we recommended they focus on the high-gain areas.

With a more advanced model focused on strategy, people, processes, and tools, we could better guide our businesses. In addition, we could better determine the marketing and sales skills necessary to be successful—which is the topic of the next chapter.

Chapter 4:
The Right Marketing and Sales Skills

A considerable challenge facing the Marketing and Sales Department consists of deciding who has what responsibilities and accountabilities. These may be directly related to pricing or indirectly related, but they're critically important to pricing optimization, i.e., segmentation, product or offering, channel, value proposition, assets, etc. (Although responsibilities and accountabilities are well defined among professional players on a football team, they aren't as obvious within an organization until you make them so. You need only watch one pee-wee football game—in which half of the children charge every ball and the other half are day dreaming—to understand the importance of clarifying responsibilities and accountabilities.)

Consider this: How do these responsibilities align with your business leaders, product-line managers, and business or centralized pricing groups? Without this clarity, you may miss important areas, overlap in others, and provide insufficient training and skill development. Remember that pricing is only one aspect of the four Ps of marketing. To achieve superior pricing and profits, these four Ps (product, promotion, place, and price) must be considered holistically, just as in football when a play is called, all the players—from the quarterback to the receivers and running backs—must work the play as one team.

That said, it's not as important *how* you distribute marketing and pricing-related responsibilities and accountabilities as it is to simply do it. Establishing clarity and alignment across the organization and ensuring you have no gaps in key responsibilities are your critical goals. Then, of course, everyone who's agreed to participate must play his or her part.

Pricing isn't accomplished by only one group or expert; it takes a village—a whole interconnected team—to set the stage for a price increase.

Roles and Responsibilities

Following is an example of the type of accountabilities and responsibilities you might consider for your marketing, sales, business, and product-line management leaders, plus your sales force. While these specific suggestions may not be right for your company—especially if you don't have all of these roles—you do need to be sure that *someone* owns each of the following critical pieces mentioned. When clarifying responsibilities within your organization, go back and refer to Play 2: Chapter 3 to assure they align with your pricing roles and organizational decision rights. Further, recognize that some of the groups (especially marketing roles) might have the accountability and decision rights for the issues discussed but will likely rely on the pricing resources to provide analysis and price recommendations.

Marketing Leaders

Typically, Marketing will be the predominate driver of price setting and broad-based price increases. Thus it's appropriate that your marketing leader(s) own and set the price targets and floor prices by segments, recommending major price increases to the business leader for final approval. And if Marketing plays this role, marketing leaders in concert with the business leader will also provide strategic risk guidance by segment. For example, they may guide the sales force to take large-volume risk with your least attractive segments (e.g., customer groups that predominately buy on price). On the other hand, they will likely not want to risk too much volume loss with your most attractive customer segments. This will guide the sales force to back off on price increases if the risk of volume loss begins to appear high.

As drivers of long-term profitability, marketing leaders need to understand their businesses' pricing power, market/customer needs, and market dynamics. Then they can assess the company's price and profitability power over the next few years and adjust the marketing strategies for optimal sustained profitability.

Marketing leaders also own the accountability to advance the pricing processes and systems as well as set sales policies, including pricing guidance, price mechanisms, payment terms, volume brackets, etc. They're responsible for (but may delegate to marketing communication resources) the creation of the internal and external pricing and value proposition communications. They may also take the lead in the quantification of value needed for good price setting and value proposition development. Please note that a talented marketing leader would always work closely with his or her sales leader counterpart and/or product-line manager to set prices, policies, and the value proposition.

WHAT IS A VALUE PROPOSITION?

A value proposition describes both the benefits that your product will provide to the customer and how your product enables this benefit, then how you will be compensated for this value. For example, your product provides the customer a 10% yield improvement based on

> your superior and patented technology and is offered at a $2/kg premium. Your value proposition is most effective when you can quantify the benefits to the customer in monetary terms and when you can credibly demonstrate the value that exists.

Lastly, if you have them, the pricing manager and pricing analyst will likely report directly or indirectly to the marketing leader. And though the marketing leader retains accountability, he or she may delegate certain responsibilities to pricing resources available. These pricing roles, as well as the corporate pricing experts, act in service to the business and marketing leaders.

Sales Leaders

Sales leaders own the execution of the pricing strategy and policies. Their role consists of working with their individual sales folks, understanding risky customer price moves, and helping sales people to set appropriate customer targets within the given pricing boundaries.

They may also rebalance customer targets (i.e., give a higher price increase to one customer and a lower increase to another to generate the same dollar impact with less risk of volume loss). In addition, they may monitor performance through price changes to assure the targets are hit within the preset time windows. They should also be the first approval line for pricing or agreement terms that don't meet targets or policies. (*Note:* Some exceptions might be elevated to market or business managers.)

Sales leaders manage the formal communications to their organization regarding pricing moves and conduct formal sales force meetings, perhaps weekly during intense price-increase periods. In these meetings, they share price wins and learnings, gather competitive intelligence, and build confidence.

In addition, sales leaders need to develop their sales force into capable value sellers so they can convincingly communicate the value of your offering and be effectively compensated for this value.

Product-line Managers

Product-line managers are the integrators between marketing and supply chain. As such, they often have a role in strategic pricing issues, such as recommending product lines or manufacturing facility changes that enhance the company's long-term pricing power. They're often the ones who gather intelligence about competitive costs, capacity, or strategy—all of which are fundamentals needed for long-term strategic pricing.

As an example, at one point in my career, I was the product manager of a product line that was being regulated out of the market over a number of years. As the market declined, most competitors were running their manufacturing assets (plants) at a low rate. Pricing was starting to suffer as competitors dropped price to gain volume and refill their assets. So I led an initiative to shut down one of our several assets (we actually retrofitted the plant to a brand new product) and agreed to manufacture product at a reasonable cost for one of our competitors. This competitor then chose to shut down its plant site. The elimination of two large assets resulted in the market demand better matching the industry capacity. This positioned us to increase our prices and, not surprising, other competitors increased their prices as well.

Because strategic pricing often results in changes to business strategy or assets, product-line managers become key players in these projects. They also need to understand product and segment profitability plus market dynamics and supply-chain capability. This knowledge helps them offer recommendations or aid business and marketing leaders in improving product, market, or customer segmentation, targeting, and differential management decisions. The goal remains the same: to optimize pricing and profitability.

Business Leader

The business leader often has the final approval on price increases, paying particular attention to strategic pricing and implications affecting business strategy. The business leader should provide high-level risk tolerance guidance regarding potential volume loss.

For example, during 2006-2007 when oil prices and many raw materials were rapidly increasing in price, many business leaders in DuPont knew they not only had a compelling case to "push" raw material increases on to their customers, but that this was imperative for their businesses to remain healthy. These leaders explicitly told people in their organization they expected them to fully achieve their price increases, even if it meant some loss of business. They explained that, given market dynamics, it was a fair and appropriate increase. Plus the increase was critical for the business to continue funding the innovation pipeline. The leaders expressed their confidence that the sales force would be successful in achieving the increases with little volume risk. They also made it clear that, as leaders, they were willing to take the accountability for losses.

A year later approaching the 2008-2009 recession, the leaders provided different risk guidance. For instance, when a price increase was justified but the competitive reaction was uncertain, one business leader guided the group to increase the price in its lowest profitability segment first. That way, they could judge the market reaction before setting the guidance for their most profitable segments.

Sales Force

The sales force must proactively understand the various needs of their customers so they can 1) modify their offering within specific business-set parameters to meet customers' needs and 2) inform the marketing and technical organizations so they can better develop compelling offerings. The sales force is also responsible for effectively negotiating price and terms with customers within the pricing targets and guidelines they're given *and commensurate with the value delivered*. They have the role of communicating with their accounts, explaining their value, justifying price moves, and making customers feel fairly treated. In addition, individual sales people must evaluate and report to management the risks they foresee to their accounts.

Training and Development

Price training and coaching as provided or recommended by the central pricing group are musts for all the roles involved in pricing. Execution of the training might include:

- *Formal courses*

- *Internal conferences or sharing sessions*

- *Email guidance or webinars*

- *Other communications, such as articles, books, or one-on-one coaching.*

Some firms offer one- or two-day pricing courses for sales and marketing/business leaders. *Advice:* Having attended many meetings of the Professional Pricing Society, Institute for the Study of Business Markets, and various consulting firms, I can attest to their quality. I found the two-day pricing course from The Monitor Group (now part of Deloitte) to be the most well rounded in all levels of pricing, making it one of my favorites for business, product-line, marketing, and sales leadership.

On the sales force side, I suggest focusing on a shorter one-day version of the same material and also considering value-selling courses or negotiation courses that focus on pricing. *Advice:* The Bay Group International offers a highly effective course called Price Pressure Negotiation.

Sales Incentives

The sales VP or director should review the company's sales incentive programs and assess whether they're likely to help, hurt, or be neutral relative to pricing effectively. If your sales people are on a full or partial commission compensation program and volume or share is a dominate factor in determining their pay, this could stifle your pricing efforts or work against you. Be sure to adjust incentives to also include profit growth (e.g., gross contribution dollars), variable contribution margin, or price as an additional key component if you are looking to optimize your price and profitability. With a few exceptions, improved profitability should trump improved share or volume. And unless you have an extremely high variable margin (i.e., 80%), you're likely to find that higher prices will deliver noticeably higher profits—even if you lose some volume to gain the higher price.

Can you imagine a quarterback having pay incentives based on the number of passes thrown rather than the number of passes successfully received? Clearly, the first incentive would be less effective in driving behavior that wins games—

the ultimate goal. Likewise, volume gains as a sales incentive without pricing/margin gains may not drive the behaviors that result in optimal profits—the ultimate business goal.

For example, if your business has a 20% variable margin—the formula is ((revenue - variable cost)/revenue)—then with a 10% price increase, you could afford to lose up to 33% of your volume and still have equal or better profits.

On the other hand, if your variable margin were 80%, you could only afford to lose up to 12% of your volume and still equal or improve your profits.

Your central pricing group should be able to provide guidance on setting up the factors for your sales incentive program. But recognize that these factors should change if the market dynamics and/or your business objectives significantly change. Having a price increase factor may make sense during times when price increases will likely succeed, but it may drive the wrong behavior during recessionary times. A variable margin percent (or unit variable margin—i.e., $/kg) might be a better metric in soft times. If you opt to use a contribution dollar metric, be sure to educate and reinforce to your sales representatives the higher impact of price over volume in generating profits.

Having addressed the roles and skills involved in your pricing game, let's move on to the third play in your playbook: getting to the right price.

PLAY 3:
THE RIGHT PRICE

If a sports team tries to play with a ball that's either overly inflated or almost deflated, the team's ability to perform will suffer. Likewise, if you inflate or deflate your prices too much, your execution and sales won't be optimal. You need to determine the right price for the highest profits.

Specifically, you want to improve your pricing effectiveness in the three predominant areas previously mentioned: *transactional* pricing, *value-in-use*, or *value* pricing, and *strategic* pricing. Most businesses need to focus on all three; however, commodity businesses may spend much less time on value-in-use pricing. All three of these areas can and should be rich in financial returns. Using our football analogy, football players need to focus on offensive skills, defensive skills, *and* special team skills. All three contribute to team success. Now any given team might balance the focus on these three areas in slightly different ways. For example, if the team has an outstanding quarterback, it's likely to have a heavier focus on its offensive skills, and particularly passing/receiving skills.

Transactional Pricing: Transactional pricing is done at the customer-by-customer level and/or transaction-by-transaction level. It involves analysis to determine where you're leaking value versus adhering to your pricing or sales policies and customer agreements, or where your pricing or sales policies and customer agreements need to be changed to eliminate undue price leakage. For example, if you charge the same price for a full truckload as you do for a drum of product, you may be missing an opportunity to charge more for the drum. Likewise, if your sales policies state you will charge an additional 2% surcharge for drums but you haven't been charging the customer this surcharge, you are leaking value. Likewise, a quarterback's play may leak value if the other players involved don't sufficiently cover the opposing team's players. These price increases often involve granular moves, customer by customer, or broad-based changes in pricing and sales policies.

If you're just getting started on improving your pricing competency, transactional pricing is easy because it requires the least amount of deep marketing information and external knowledge. You'll be off and running if you have good analytical skills and a bit of marketing guidance. Plus, you'll likely achieve the big, quick wins in this area.

Value-in-Use (or Value) Pricing: Perhaps the most complex and difficult to execute of the three approaches, value-in-use pricing requires more of the organization's involvement and more marketing savvy to implement. It also potentially takes the longest time to reap the benefits. That said, value-in-use pricing is the ultimate holy grail of pricing, so do go for it. In football, no doubt the top players command higher compensation than the other players by making clear the unique value they bring to the team. Why shouldn't you ask higher prices for products that deliver significant value to your customers?

Value-in-use (or value) pricing is often accomplished at a customer segment or market segment level (or a combination of both). It involves a deep understanding of the value your products and services bring relative to the customer's next best alternative and the needs the customer is willing to pay for. In segments for which you offer additional value, you target price premiums to capture this value at the segment and/or individual customer level. If you have a product that provides the customer a higher heat resistance than competitive products, you should be charging more for this product to the end users that get the benefit from this higher heat resistance. For instance, this may be of high value in automotive or electrical markets but have little value when sold for cosmetic applications. You will want to slightly modify your offering (i.e., create slight differences in product, services, and/or packaging) if you plan on selling it to different markets at two different price points.

Strategic Pricing: In my opinion, strategic pricing is the next place to focus after transactional pricing. Although it requires a high level of business and marketing experience, it can deliver a broad-based financial impact. It's also among the fastest and least complex types of price increases to implement.

Strategic pricing is determined at an industry or market level. At this level, you evaluate industry dynamics and the competitive environment to identify, and possibly influence, favorable industry/market dynamics for pricing (for example, tight supply and demand balance industry-wide). When favorable dynamics exist, it's time to set broad-based price increases across the full industry or market segments. Price-related behaviors—price moves, communications, and reactions to competitive actions—should consistently contribute to positive industry pricing dynamics.

Admittedly, these behaviors show little similarity to behaviors in a specific football game because strategic pricing is about creating a win-win situation. But we can look for actions that enhance the entire league's ability to draw more sponsors and fans—a situation in which all teams win. And we can look for actions that avoid behavior such as player strikes, which could discourage followers—a situation in which all teams lose. Just as some actions (such as playing fair) enhance the entire sport of football, strategic pricing creates a scenario that supports an entire industry.

One of our DuPont businesses had a practice of running its manufacturing plant full out. Excess capacity was used to make a low-value commodity product. This excess product was sent to Asia and sold at distressed prices. When the central pricing team evaluated this business strategy, it quickly realized the practice was disruptive to the overall market pricing and contributed to lower market prices rather than fair value. We helped the business leaders understand the fair value and recommended they stop their practice of always running the plant at full capacity, then selling excess product at low prices. We also recommended they raise prices and communicate their value and new strategy to their market/customer base. By consistently following this practice, they made significant price increases that far, far out-valued the extra opportunistic volume they left behind.

Pricing Projects

In my experience, a project-by-project approach is the best way to tackle these three areas of pricing.

Projects are led by your central pricing experts (even if they're still-emerging experts), often focused on just one of these three areas at a time. As you advance, your pricing projects are likely to have elements of all three. Over time, you can expect the businesses' pricing roles (staff) to become fairly strong in transactional pricing and possibly some elements of either strategic or value pricing.

However, it's highly unlikely they will both develop the depth of skill and have the time to do full justice to strategic and value-in-use pricing. This, then, proves to be the main advantage of a dedicated group of centralized experts. The group can periodically (once or twice a year) lead a deeper analysis within your businesses or product lines to supplement the day-to-day business pricing efforts. Just as football scouts bring in deep knowledge of competitive teams and players to enhance their team's strategy, so can the central pricing group dedicate time to gathering extensive competitive and market intelligence to enhance pricing strategies.

So what might a project look like? While it typically depends on the scope of the project and the complexity of the business, a good rule of thumb for the project team might be linking two to three folks from the central group with two to three from the business. On the central team, one senior manager who leads the project and one or two analysts essentially dedicate themselves full time to the project. The business resources depend on the type of project but, in general, those who contribute most (i.e., +/-50% of their time) are likely to be the pricing manager, an analyst (i.e., pricing, financial, Six Sigma black belt expert), and the product-line manager or market manager. Others will get involved periodically as needed. These projects typically are scoped to last three to four months.

Chapters 5, 6, and 7 address the basics of transactional, value pricing, and strategic projects. They'll focus on practical ways to get started and accelerate your financial benefits. Although this book doesn't delve into the deep theoretical background of these pricing areas, many books on the market do. (See *The Strategy and Tactics of Pricing* by Tom Nagle and John Hogan, for example.)

Basic Fundamentals of Pricing Decisions

As you begin your pricing analyses, you'll use variable margin as the predominate basis for analyzing profit and making pricing decisions. True fixed costs are generally ignored under the assumption that, in the short term, they're unchangeable. So, if you change the product mix or decide on price/volume trade-offs, you'll have no change in the fixed cost to the business.

Remember, profits in the short term only change according to price, volume, and variable cost implications. Furthermore, it can be difficult to get true fixed costs at a granular level. Many accounting systems simply allocate fixed costs across products, which means that all products get equally burdened with the fixed cost. In reality, you may have some products that require more time, extra manpower, or extra equipment to produce and thus actually have a higher fixed cost then the other products. Thus it can be misleading to use fixed costs at a granular level unless you're sure of them.

Over time, fixed costs can often be partially or fully reduced. So it's worth understanding your fixed costs—especially at an aggregate level (by plant site, product line, etc.)—to ensure all elements of the business are fully profitable. If they're not, you likely need to make improvement decisions regarding your long-term business strategy, supply chain, or product line. This may require you to restructure and reduce or eliminate costs where possible. These items can be tackled in your long-term strategic pricing projects.

Two cautions: First, when dealing with variable costs, be sure to capture all of them and properly assign them to products. Many cost systems may have some "true variable costs" hidden within their fixed-cost structure. For example, tolling fees (fees you pay to a contract manufacturer to produce product for you) based on volume and strictly for a specific product, might show up in your fixed costs but should be treated as variable costs assigned only to that specific product because the volume is variable.

Second—and it's a big one—is to understand your opportunity costs. These are opportunities you'll have to forgo if you make certain customer deals. They're typically associated with constrained assets or supply (e.g., assets that are fully running and thus can't produce any more product or supply of a critical raw material that's limited and thus you can't obtain more of it).

For example, if your supply is constrained and you accept a low-price order that uses up your remaining capacity, you risk not being able to accept future orders on higher-profit deals. You've lost the opportunity to go after high-value business. So if you're in a tight supply-and-demand situation, expect to be in a tight situation shortly, or are typically tight across a normal business cycle, be sure to consider the opportunity costs.

Under these circumstances, rather than using only variable margin ($/volume unit, e.g., $/lb), you're advised to also consider variable margin *per constraint* ($/time on the constrained asset; $/constrained raw material when a given raw material is limited). Don't assume that $/unit volume directly correlates to $/constraint. This is likely to be true only if all your products run through your constrained assets at the exact same rate (e.g., 10 lbs/hour) or use the exact same percent of the constrained raw material (e.g., 5% ingredient X is contained in all finished products).

What happens if you don't consider opportunity costs? You run the risk of sub-optimizing your total profits during constrained times.

Opportunity costs differ from variable margin when the constraint (i.e., asset capacity or raw material availability) is not equally apportioned across products. Thus, if different products run at different rates in a capacity-limited asset (e.g., product "A" runs at 5 lbs/hour and product "B" runs at 10 lbs/hour), products generated faster will produce more volume to sell during the same timeframe (i.e., product B will produce twice as much volume in a year than product A). This potentially allows higher profits, presuming you can sell this additional product.

Likewise, different products may use a different percent of the constrained raw material. In that case, products requiring a lower percentage of the constrained raw material will allow you to generate more volume with the same amount of the limited raw material than one requiring a higher percentage. This, again, potentially allows higher profits.

In the end, consider the combination of $/unit product (e.g., $/kg) multiplied by the production rate (e.g., product kgs/time or product kgs/raw material kgs of constrained raw material). *When you have constraints to your supply,* that is the key measure to optimize; it's a critical issue in price/volume trade-off decisions, product-mix decisions, and product rationalization decisions.

Price/Volume Trade-off

Do you go for a seven-point touchdown or a three-point field goal? Do you punt or go for the down? These are risky trade-off decisions that must be optimized to win a game. It takes skill, courage, and leadership to decide the best course of action. Likewise in pricing, you must make risky trade-off decisions hoping to deliver superior profits. Do you raise price and risk losing volume? Do you lower the price hoping you will gain more volume? Do you drop price to match a competitor? Here, too, deciding takes skill, courage, and leadership.

No matter what type of pricing project you're involved in, it's critical to think about the price/volume trade-off of your decisions.

That means anytime you increase price, you run the risk of losing volume. Likewise, anytime you drop price, you increase the potential of gaining volume. (I say the *potential* because often the competitor that currently has the business will drop price to match yours, so you don't end up with more volume.) Therefore, focus on understanding the price/volume break-even point, or the break-even volume. That's the volume you can afford to lose if you're increasing price—or the volume you must gain if you're dropping price to be neutral on profits.

The Strategy and Tactics of Pricing by Thomas Nagle and John Hogan offers a simple, easy calculation to do this: *The break-even volume equals the negative change in price percent divided by the sum of the variable margin percent and the change in price percent.*[1]

BREAK-EVEN VOLUME CALCULATION WHEN RAISING OR LOWERING PRICE

BE Volume = - (% Change in Price) / (% Variable Margin + % Change in Price)

For example, if you're considering a 10% price increase on a 30% variable-margin business (-10%/(30%+10%) = -25%), you can afford to lose as much as 25% of your volume. Should you lose more than 25%, you will hurt your profitability. Should you lose less than 25%, you will create additional profits.

This quick math takes seconds to do but can be powerful in removing emotion and fear from a conversation and turning it to effective, logical thinking. It's specifically designed for proactive moves in the market; don't attempt to use it when responding to a competitive threat.

1   Thomas Nagle and John Hogan. *The Strategy and Tactics of Pricing.* Pearson Prentice Hall; 4th edition, 2005. p. 178.

Along with the break-even calculation, you'll want to consider "spillover effects." As an example, suppose you're raising prices on a product and it becomes transparent in the marketplace. This move may have a bonus—a *positive* spillover effect—of contributing to favorable industry pricing that allows you to more easily raise prices on other products.

Likewise, if you drop price and it becomes transparent in the marketplace, this can have *negative* spillover effect. The price drop might result in other customers asking for price decreases or in competitors following your price decrease to prevent you from gaining share from their accounts. Whichever way you go, be particularly thoughtful when decreasing price; it can be highly disruptive to the overall market price.

Next, let's tackle the details of the three pricing approaches: transactional, value, and strategic pricing.

Chapter 5:
Transactional Price Setting

As briefly explained earlier, transactional price setting involves analysis to determine where your business is leaking value from not adhering to your price targets and/or sales policies or from having weak sales policies. So ask yourself: Are you executing your pricing well, and/or do your pricing and sales policies need to be changed to eliminate undue price leakage?

Remember, this analysis is conducted at the most granular of levels: customer/product by customer/product and even, at times, transaction by transaction. Price increases often involve either highly focused moves—customer by customer—or broad-based changes in pricing and sales policies.

Transactional price setting is one of the best ways to ease into pricing excellence—a great way to crawl before you walk. Why? Because it requires fewer marketing, pricing, and external skills than value and strategic pricing. With just one or two marketing/pricing experts and strong analytical resources, you can get started. And odds are, if you haven't focused on this transactional area in the past, you will achieve solid financial benefits. This endeavor will give the pricing group quick wins to gain credibility with corporate and business leadership. You can quite reasonably expect a 1-3% revenue uplift as pre-tax earnings (which translates into 10-30% pre-tax earnings depending on your cost position). Not a bad way to make a good impression!

If you don't have a few strong pricing experts in the company to get started, don't let that stop you. Outside firms such as Deloitte will work with your "experts in training" to execute projects and help develop your experts. While this does mean spending more of your budget, the returns will make it an excellent decision. You'll accelerate your learning curve while accelerating your financial gains.

Even if you do have strong pricing experts, it might be wise to bring in an outside pricing firm for at least one project to test whether your experts' skill levels are as deep as you think. I suspect that, whether you are using experienced marketing experts or recent MBA graduates, you'll find there's much they can learn from external pricing consultants.

In your analysis of transactional pricing, you can use the following checklist to determine areas of focus when looking for price leakage.

Price Leakage Checklist

Customer-by-Customer Pricing

- *Price variance: Which customers and products are below your price targets or noticeably lower in price then others? Is there a wide spread of prices and if so, is it justified?*

- *Price by account size: Do any small customers enjoy the same low prices as larger customers?*

- *Package size or order size discounts: Are you providing discounts for small order sizes? Do you price lower for large shipping containers such as trucks versus pallets or drums and price higher for a single drum or can? Are your policies for packages or order volume discounts designed effectively?*

- *Volume threshold: Do your contracts have minimum-volume purchase requirements to receive lower prices or price discounts? If so, are these set effectively, are*

*they clear in the contracts, and are the thresholds being
achieved to earn the discount?*

Product and Regional Mix

- *Product mix: Can you modify the product mix you sell
  to achieve a more profitable mix? (Be sure to consider
  opportunity cost and maximize your $/time if you're sold
  out or typically sold out during your usual business cycle.)*

- *Regional mix: Can you shift your sales among regions for
  a higher profitability blend? Can you raise prices in lower
  profitability regions to achieve better global alignment?*

- *Channel mix: Can you shift your sales to different selling
  channels (e.g., distribution, selling agents, direct sales,
  online sales) as a way to improve profitability?*

- *Supply mix: Do some products run much slower or
  incur much more cost on some assets? If so, can you
  shift these products between manufacturing or contract
  manufacturing sites to improve your cost position or
  improve your capacity?*

Payment Terms

- *Early payment terms: Are some customers receiving early
  payment terms? Any greater than 1%? Are they actually
  earning their discounts by paying early?*

- *Payment term variance: Do you have a lot of unnecessary
  variance in your pricing term length? Any customers
  receiving over 30 days net?*

- *Late payments: Do you have penalties for late payments?
  If so, do you adhere to your policies? Do some customers
  consistently pay late?*

Cost to Service

- *Freight: Are you charging for air freight, expedited shipments, or rush orders? Do you charge for less-than-full truckloads or less-than-full pallet shipments? Do you offer discounts to give customers incentive to buy in bulk or consolidate orders? Do you specify minimum order or shipment quantities? If you have these policies, are you adhering to them?*

- *Product rationalization: Can you raise the price significantly on small/low-profit products to capture sufficient value or should you exit the product? If exiting a product, can you do so by raising the price significantly, thus testing whether you've underestimated its value?*

- *Customization: Are you charging extra in price or surcharges for custom requests? Custom products, special packaging, special labeling, extra lab testing or analysis, extra paper requirements?*

- *Product scheduling: Are your make-to-order and make-to-stock product scheduling segmentation and policies creating value or extra costs?*

- *Packaging-size pricing: Are certain packages less profitable? Should you have fewer package choices or higher prices on more unique package choices?*

- *Order changes: Do your policies or practices result in costly order alterations, cancellations, or returns?*

- *Equipment and services: Are you fairly compensated for any services or equipment rentals you provide? Are you compensated for disposal/recycle services, equipment installation or calibration, maintenance, unique prototyping/tooling or product development you might provide at a customer's request?*

- *Consulting and Other services: Are you fairly compensated for services such as customer productivity improvement assessments, audits, training, or co-marketing efforts?*

- *Systems interlinking: Do you have any systems that are connected to customers, such as vendor inventory management, maintenance/operation monitoring, or logistics management? Are you compensated?*

- *Selling and ordering services: Do you provide any special services, such as single point of contact or a special 24-hour hotline?*

Agreement Management

- *Price openers: Do you have price openers in your agreements that allow you to change price within 30-90 days?*

- *Policies: Are your sales policies clearly defined in your customer agreements? Do you use standard agreements with customers?*

- *Length: Do your informal and formal agreements have a clearly defined timeframe? Does your system record and notify you of the agreement end date?*

Processes and Practices

- *Pricing setting and approval: Do you have a high-quality formal process that you adhere to? Do prices that fall below your target or floor prices require formal review and approval?*

- *Contract adherence: Do you monitor your contracts to ensure customers are paying the appropriate price for products and services per contract terms?*

- *Pricing performance: Do you monitor your pricing performance sufficiently? Do you take actions when you see defects?*

Getting Started

Scope out your project. I suggest you start with one region and one business line, preferably one that's motivated to work with you. Pull together your team. Perhaps start with one high-level pricing expert to lead the project and two analysts from the central pricing group who are dedicated essentially full time to the project for 8 to 12 weeks. The business will then need to add resources, including at least one analyst nearly full time and at least 30% dedication from a product-line or marketing manager acting as the business lead. Additional support might be needed from Finance or IT (10-20% in the initial weeks) to gather data, as well as 5% from other commercial managers periodically.

Step 1: Begin collecting the standard profitability data (specifics follow). If your data systems aren't efficient or the quality of the data is weak, this step can take three to six weeks to collect, cleanse, and validate. Not fun work, but the basis of your analysis must be credible to the organization to get the buy-in to act on your recommendations.

As you collect data, continue to work on other parts of the project.

Standard data includes granular customer/product profitability data (i.e., list price or targets, actual price, variable cost, freight cost, and volume) for one year in monthly increments at a minimum. (Depending on the nature of your business, you might extend this data to transaction by transaction, although most businesses can avoid this level of detail.) Also collect data on payment terms, rebates, other discounts, and market, customer and/or regional segmentation.

Step 2: While you gather data, begin formal interviews (8 to 10) of the commercial team: business leader, market manager(s), sales leader, product-line manager, and one or two customer service representatives. Design your questionnaire around questions such as:

- *How often do you raise price in a year? Are the increases successful? Why or why not?*

- *How are price targets set, and how are actual customer-specific prices and terms approved?*

- *What are your sales policies related to payment terms, minimum order quantities, volume price brackets, etc.? Do you adhere to your policies?*

- *Do you offer rebates, special discounts, or tiered pricing? How are these set and administered?*

- *Do you take customer size, package container, or order size into account when setting prices, discounts, or rebates?*

- *Are your more unique products priced higher than standard products?*

- *Do you sell direct to customers or through distributors or agents? What is the payment mechanism used for distributors or agents?*

- *Where do you think you might be leaking price value?*

- *What is your market share and how has it been changing over the last few years?*

- *Have you seen any changes in the market dynamics over the past year or so (e.g., changes in supply/demand balance, competitive activity, customer needs, etc.)?*

Step 3: With the interviews and any early data collected in hand, begin to hypothesize areas of price leakage and opportunities to capture value. Be sure your data collection plan is robust enough to answer all your hypotheses. If it is not, then expand your data collection. Keep your hypotheses list ever-green; add to it or remove items as you learn more.

Step 4: Conduct an in-depth exploratory analysis of the data collected. This analysis is likely to include the standard analysis listed below but also customized analysis based on your price leakage hypotheses. Typical analysis might include:

- *Waterfall charts: A waterfall chart starts with list price and shows the leakage, in buckets, to reach the final net price then net variable margin. Leakage buckets would include items such as discounts (market, volume, order-size discounts), rebates, distributor charges, prototypes/tooling costs, expedited freight, early payment terms, variable costs, and variable service charges. (See Figure 2.)*

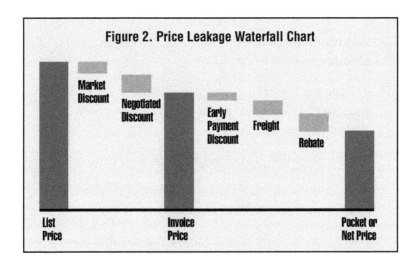

Figure 2. Price Leakage Waterfall Chart

- *Price or variable-margin scatter plots: A scatter plot is an X-Y axis graph with individual data points plotted or "scattered" on it. Plot the price and/or variable margin (Y axis) versus volume (X axis) for each customer or each product (SKU level). (See Figure 3.) The scattered data points will show visible patterns and reveal:*

  - *if smaller products or customers have higher price or margin as you would expect them to;*

  - *if the price or margin spread for a given volume is fairly tight or small, as you would expect from a business with good pricing discipline and price approval processes; and*

  - *if any customer or product appears to be well below the others, indicating a potentially easy area to improve price.*

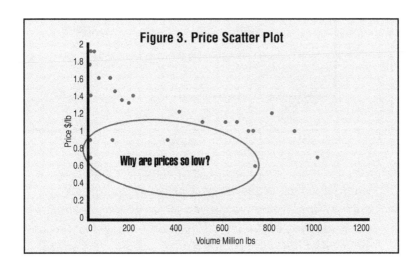

Figure 3. Price Scatter Plot

- *Variable margin versus total contribution scatter plots: At a product bulk or family level, plot variable margin on the Y axis and contribution dollars on the X axis. Divide the graph into a matrix of four quadrants. The upper right quadrant includes your "All-Stars" (i.e., your most attractive customers or products); the lower left includes your 'free agents" (i.e., your least attractive customers or products). Set up strategies for each quadrant—e.g., a growth strategy for the upper left quadrant, a refinement strategy for the lower right quadrant, a protect-and-grow strategy for your All-Stars, and a fix-it-or-leave-it strategy for your free agents. (See Figure 4.)*

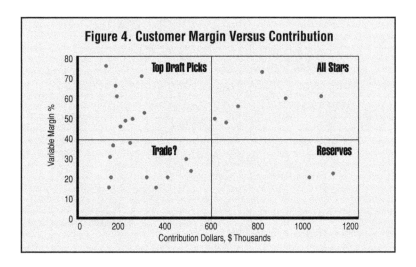

Figure 4. Customer Margin Versus Contribution

- *Price bands or box plots: A price band is a graphical method to look at the range of prices for specific groups, such as similar-size customers, same product, or similar-sized shipping containers. A box plot is much like the price band but also visually depicts the quartiles within the bands (i.e., the median value, the top 25%, etc.). Your Y axis might be the price per SKU. The X axis could be the size of the customer. So for example, you might have a band for very large, large, medium, small, and tiny customers. You'd look for leakage from small customers that are enjoying the same low price as large customers. You can also do versions in which the X axis is order quantity (e.g., trucks, drums, pails) or segments such as market, customer, or region. (See Figure 5.)*

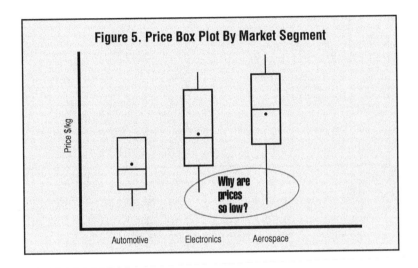

- *Revenue or profit velocity charts by product: Plot the cumulative revenue or profit by product from the largest to the smallest. (See Figure 6.) Typically 80% of your profits or revenue will come from 20% of the products. Do you have a large number of products that bring in very little revenue or profit? If so, they may be creating complexity with no meaningful profit uplift. Can you increase their price or exit these products? Don't worry about new products that are expected to substantially grow.*

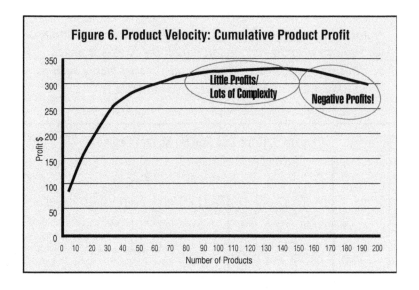

Figure 6. Product Velocity: Cumulative Product Profit

- *Adherence to policy analysis: Analyze actual performance with respect to policies; for example, are you charging for expedited shipments according to your policy?*

- *Price monthly trends: Plot one to three years of pricing trends by segment to see if patterns exist (seasonal, quarter-end spikes, year-end spikes).*

If you have the data, do these analyses by market, customer, or region breakdowns. With the visuals you've created and others you may opt to perform, begin to test and confirm your price leakage hypotheses.

Step 5: Finalize your conclusions on price leakage areas and improvement recommendations. What policies or practices should be changed or added? Do you need to improve adherence to policy? What price increases should you consider?

Have working sessions with the business team or select commercial leaders to jointly identify new opportunities or solutions.

Step 6: Finalize the process with a steering team review, which includes top commercial leadership. Get agreement on which recommendations the business is committed to implementing. Agree on the responsible person(s) and timing for implementation.

The more projects you do—especially if they're across diverse business lines and regions—the faster and more effective your experts will become. Once you've covered many of your businesses and regions, it's time to think about turning the majority of this type of pricing over to the businesses. On an 80/20 basis, they should be managing these aspects of pricing.

However, accomplishing that isn't as easy as saying, "It's yours; go to it." You'll likely need to invest in system upgrades to facilitate easy and credible data collection as well as have standard monthly analyses or graphs generated. These actions must be combined with clarity from the businesses on their pricing roles and responsibilities.

Like a sports team, you need to plan a variety of plays to address different situations. Some plans aren't as easy to execute as others—but keep your pricing plays at the ready for when you need them.

The next chapter addresses a more difficult approach to pricing—one that takes into consideration not just the product or service itself but the perceived value of the product, which can vary between customer and market groups.

Chapter 6:
Value Price Setting

Value pricing involves a deep understanding of the value your products and services bring relative to the customer's next best alternative and the needs the customer is willing to pay for you to meet. Ideally, you target price *premiums* to capture this value for cases in which you provide special value for particular customers or segments.

While value pricing can be done at the granular level (i.e., for a given product and customer), it's often more practically done at a customer-segment or market-segment level, or a combination of both. It incorporates the art and the science of quantifying your value relative to your customer's next best alternative, then setting the pricing to capture your fair share of that value.

This sounds so easy to say; why is it so hard to achieve?

Let's look at a few of the challenges (or perceived challenges) businesses often face in this arena. They have difficulty:

- *quantifying the value of their products: "The customer won't tell me." "It's subjective."*

- *quantifying the value of services, relationships, brand: "These can't be quantified with hard numbers."*

- *determining how to split the value with the customer: "Why can't we just split it 50/50?"*

- *quantifying the value across a highly complex product line: "We have too many products to do value pricing. It would takes us years. We don't have the manpower."*

- *segmenting their customers based on their customers'*
  needs: "We tried that in the past and it didn't work."
  "We've given all our services to all our customers in the
  past; we can't pull back services to some groups now that
  they're used to receiving them for free."

And those are difficulties in setting the price alone. Once it's set, you still have the challenge of convincing your customers of your product's value. That requires a lot of new training, communication packages, value-selling tools, and cultural change for your sales force.

To make major headway against these challenges, your marketing, pricing, and even technology/technical service leaders as well as your sales force must work together proactively. There's plenty of heavy lifting to go around, and you'd best not underestimate managing the cultural change that's required. Being true value sellers is hard work and often quite different work from the selling your organization is used to conducting. (Again, read *Value Merchants* by John C. Anderson, Nirmalya Kumar, and James A. Narus to get a flavor of the change management and effort involved in becoming a truly value-based pricing organization.)

As nearly always happens with pricing efforts, the view at the top is worth the climb. You will enhance not only your pricing but your volume growth. The return on this effort will come; it just may take longer than some of your strategic or transactional pricing moves.

That said, you have easy ways to start the journey and begin to capture value. I find it best to think about and approach value pricing in phases—from very basic levels to more advanced levels.

Value Pricing Levels of Advancement

From a value-selling advancement standpoint or ease of implementation, the following four phases progress from basic and easy to sophisticated and challenging to implement.

1. **Emerging—product-by-product approach:** Quantify your value for specific select products (e.g., new products or select unique products) and set their target prices. Develop basic value communication messages. Train the sales force on value-selling techniques.

2. **Established—product by product with tools approach:** Develop value-selling tools such as value calculators that allow a sales person to customize the value quantification to the specific customer situation.

3. **Advanced—segmentation and offering design:** Segment your customers, design different offerings with different prices that align with the needs of each segment, and then execute this differential approach.

4. **Very advanced—holistic value-seller culture, practices, systems:** Develop a holistic value-selling culture and approach; facilitate it with a holistic set of value-selling tools that aid you in customer needs identification, value quantification, offering/price development, and communication/negotiation packages.

As they are implemented, each of these phases will bring in increasing value. All are built on the basics of value selling, described as follows.

The Basics of Value Price Setting

Following are the necessary steps to set a well thought-out value-based price. Once you see what they are, we'll get into more detail. (Refer to Figure 7.)

1. Identify the next best alternative(s) your customer(s) would consider as an alternative to buying your offering.

2. Brainstorm all the possible advantages your offering might bring the customer above and beyond what the next best alternative would bring. Consider advantages that provide the customer lower cost, higher revenue, peace of mind, lower risk, or improved cash flow (e.g., less inventory, delayed capital expenditures). Think about both the *features* of your offering and the *benefits* the customer derives from these features. For example, your product might have *higher quality* that will result in the customer achieving *higher yield*.

3. Identify all the possible disadvantages your offering might have relative to your customer's next best alternative.

4. Separate those advantages and disadvantages into those that can be quantified, at least in theory (e.g., improves yield by X%, improves customer's product quality by Y%) and are subjective (e.g., improves relationship, avoids risk to switch to a new supplier, improves aesthetics).

5. Now for the hard part: Quantify each of the non-subjective advantages and disadvantages. First quantify the actual benefits (e.g., 20% improved quality, 10% improved yield), then quantify what

that benefit is worth to the customer (e.g., \$Y/ kg in revenue from price premium, \$X/kg of reduced cost).

6. Using the next best alternative price as a base, add all the extra value you bring, and subtract the cost of your disadvantages. The gap between the next best alternative price and this result is the value gap. Set your price within this gap band in such a way that you split the value with your customer.

7. Look to your subjective advantages and disadvantages to help you determine what share of the gap you retain and what share your customers retain. The more subjective advantages you have, the more likely you will retain 50% or more of the value gap. Just remember, if you try to keep all of the gap, your customer will have zero incentive to buy from you.

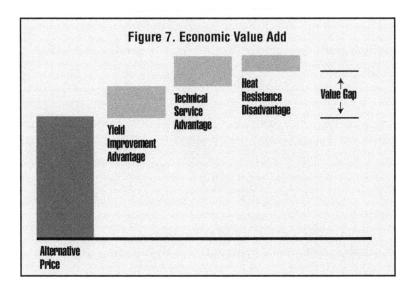

Figure 7. Economic Value Add

Conduct this analysis with a specific customer or customer segment in mind. Different market segments and customer needs-based segments within each market segment will likely have different needs and thus different values. If you try to price the same for all segments, you'll be underpricing for some segments (leaking pricing profits) and overpricing for other segments (leaking volume profits).

Quantifying Your Value and Your Value Segments

Many techniques are available to quantify value, and some of these techniques are also helpful in determining whether different value segments exist for your company. For example, some market or customer segments may value that your product is heat resistant and you offer technical support. Other segments may not care about heat resistance and technical support and thus are unwilling to pay for these features. At times, quantifying your value is easy and straightforward, but when it's difficult or you're also trying to establish the different value segments, consider reaching out to an external consulting firm that excels in value pricing and/or segmentation. (As mentioned previously, I've found the Deloitte-Monitor group to be a good choice.)

Your first step is to generate your value hypotheses, preferably with a cross-functional team from your sales, technology, technical service, marketing, and customer service areas. If you're developing value-based segments, you'll need to also develop hypotheses on the product or service features that might have different value to different groups. Then you need to gather at least internal views and quite possibly external views to validate and refine your hypotheses.

Consider these possible approaches:

Internal value assessments: Analyze the value either subjectively or by means of a thorough economic value-add analysis validated by your sales, marketing, and technical leaders. Subjectively might mean your group believes that, given your value hypothesis, you can garner a 3-5% premium. A thorough analysis would mean to actually quantify each value feature using your best estimates of customer value.

This internal value assessment approach works best for products with low differentiation or small-volume mature products—largely because these products might not justify the expense and time necessary for deeper assessments. As the product differentiation increases, or if the customer base doesn't perceive the value, you'll have to conduct deeper economic valuations and possibly external assessments.

External-feature value assessments: Some important value drivers or features may be quite difficult to quantify (or even identify) without customer input. Here are tips on getting this information from your customer base.

Quantifying Value Tips

- *Have your sales or technical people talk to your customers about the value of your products. Go beyond people in the procurement department, as they are unlikely to fully understand your product's value, plus it's not in their best interest to tell you. If the benefits are expected to be in the customer's cost, see if you can meet with the technical or operations personnel. If the benefits are projected to uplift revenue, then talk to the commercial team. Ask questions such as: "If our product could improve yield, would that be of value to you? Why? How much yield loss do you typically have? What would 5% improvement be worth to you? How would you measure the improvement?"*

- *Ask customers if they would be willing to provide you with performance data on your product (e.g., improved yield by X%) or allow your resources to come to their location and measure the benefits. If needed, offer them something in exchange for providing this data. For example, you might offer on-site technical support for the product startup, a 2% price drop for six months, or product exclusivity for three months.*

- *For benefits that are hard to quantify, such as technical service support, brand value, etc., you may opt to add something modest, such as a 5% premium.*

Customer interviews: Interview a handful of customers, at least five, or a larger number of customers, say 25, depending on your objective. If your objective is to understand different market or customer value segments, you'll need to interview the higher number of customers. Focus the discussion on confirming your value hypothesis. Get the customers' point of view. Our product improves the customer yield; how would *you (the customer)* measure this improvement and the benefits from the improvement? Why is that benefit important to you? How much benefit have you seen? Are there any other features or services you would value?

Customer validation is best used when designing or launching new differentiated offerings and/or for existing large-volume differentiated products.

Conjoint analysis or value mapping: A number of surveying techniques such as conjoint analysis and value mapping can help you understand the value feature by feature or the total value opposite competitors. Conjoint analysis is also frequently used to identify different customer needs-based segments.

Often electronic, these conjoint analysis or value mapping surveys might go out to 25 customers or hundreds or even thousands. The responses provide good information regarding customer trade-off choices. For instance, would the customer rather have more technical support or lower cost—

or would the customer rather buy from you at a higher price with technical service or buy from a specific competitor with no technical service?

These surveys are best used for:

- *understanding trade-off needs for a portfolio of products and services to help you both segment your customer needs and design your offerings for each segment, or*

- *comparing a specific product or product/service offerings to specific competitor offerings.*

Surveys can be especially helpful for hard-to-quantify benefits or emotional/psychological benefits (e.g., peace of mind, aesthetics, image). However, be aware they have a bias toward undervaluing the offerings, especially if your product is innovative enough that the customer has never experienced the benefits. The odds of undervaluing the offering increase if customers can't fully envision/experience the benefits.

Design of experiment: In this model, you price differentially in small pilot regions/markets to test the price/volume point. This technique is used more frequently in a B2C (business to consumer) environment with an extensive customer base, which typically has a steeper price/volume elasticity than a B2B (business to business) environment has.

Getting Started

One of the easiest ways to get started is to begin doing value pricing on all your new or emerging products. You'll likely have few enough of these to easily get your arms around, and this will help you build your competency and confidence. Then extend this work to a few of your larger, more unique products.

I've found it helpful for a business to have one of the central pricing experts hold a half-to-full-day workshop with a cross-section of a business's commercial and technical team to:

- *develop the draft of the business's value and value proposition (i.e., its hypothesis) and*

- *set a plan to fill the gaps in information needed to confirm and quantify their value.*

This facilitated approach can both stretch the thinking of the business team and stimulate creative techniques to quantify the value. In addition to value pricing knowledge, your expert facilitator should have strong strategic and marketing capabilities to achieve the best results.

I've seen many smart business folks try to follow good value-in-use pricing techniques without the use of a trained pricing expert. Although they were quite proud of the higher price point they justified, within 10 to 20 minutes of talking to them, I often uncovered significant value (even double or triple the price at times) that they left on the table. They may have gained nine yards, but they could have gained more than twice as many!

In one example, the business had successfully priced a new product 20% higher than its standard products—a real coup for them. As I talked it through with the folks, it became apparent they could have asked for closer to 60% price premium. They were shocked. Their immediate reaction? "Our customers would never pay this! They've never paid more than 20% premium on any of our new products."

It didn't take long, though, to witness what I suspected would happen. They were, indeed, successfully penetrating the market (not surprisingly as they were significantly undervaluing the product), and competition was rapidly dropping price to minimize share loss. Also not surprisingly, competitors appeared to know they couldn't compete unless they were priced significantly below that business's price. So in the end, the market shifted toward the 60% value gap but at a much lower price point. The business's underpricing inadvertently resulted in market-price depression.

In another example, a business within DuPont was asked to develop a unique material by an equipment manufacturer who had developed a unique design and was targeting its equipment for a special application. Our ability to develop this material was critical for the success of this application, and the material was expected to be about 20% of the cost of the final equipment. The business asked me to review their pricing proposal before they entered into the development agreement with the equipment manufacturer.

On the positive side, they had factored in a small price premium based on the uniqueness of our to-be-developed product; however, I pointed out it was still far, far underpriced. As it turned out, the final end-use value to the equipment manufacturer's customer was extraordinarily high, and the equipment manufacturer would have the only offering in the industry to meet the end customer's needs—that is, provided DuPont was successful with our material development. Thus the equipment manufacturer would be able to price far above their normal price.

The business's first reaction was this: "But this manufacturer is a cost-plus pricer, not a value pricer." I suggested our people work with the manufacturer to help its people see the light. I also suggested an alternative (although less ideal) approach: Price the material such that you receive the higher of a) an attractive price premium such as 30% or b) 25% of the equipment manufacturer's price. Then, if the equipment manufacturer is successful in achieving the far higher prices I believed it deserved, we would also benefit. Ultimately, the business was successful in getting the equipment manufacturer to understand the value they would collectively create. From there, they conducted more value-based negotiations.

QUICK-HIT IDEA

You might start by categorizing all your products into three buckets (with the help of the product manager or sales): undifferentiated, slightly differentiated, and differentiated. Once the products are placed into one of the three categories, analyze the actual price and margin for each bucket as well as each product within these three value buckets.

Are you capturing more price and margin for your slightly differentiated group and even more for your unique products? If not, start with a modest price increase on your differentiated product groups—for example, raise the price 5% on your slightly differentiated products and 10% on your unique products. (See Figure 8.)

Over time, you can raise the price premium once you quantify the actual value.

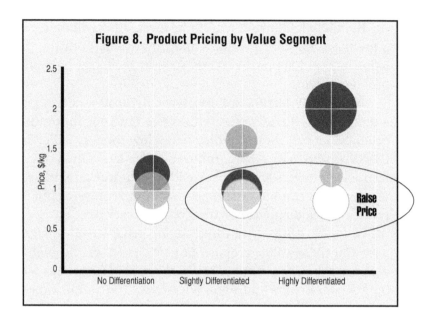

Figure 8. Product Pricing by Value Segment

Segmentation and Value Pricing

Many companies understand they have different market segments with different needs and thus can potentially vary price according to these markets. But I suggest segmentation goes beyond *market* segmentation and into *customer* segmentation.

In most markets, you'll find various customer needs-based buying groups. In my experience with numerous B2B businesses, quite often at least three types of buying groups typically emerge: price buyers, relationship buyers, and technology buyers.

Price buyers are generally unwilling to pay for anything except the basic product (although they will take all the free service they can get), and they will switch suppliers for lower price.

Relationship buyers tend to be loyal. They willingly pay a premium for your products and often value both the relationship and support services such as technical help and problem solving.

Technology buyers are also typically loyal and will pay a premium. Generally, they're interested in your innovative products or your brand, which will allow them to differentiate themselves as quality/innovation leaders. Often, these technology buyers have little need for technical support services such as troubleshooting, so you can remove technical service and add application development services.

Not surprising, these three buying groups tend to align with the three value propositions discussed in the highly acclaimed business book *The Discipline of Market Leaders* by Michael Treacy and Fred Wiersema. You would expect companies with business models that center on being a low-cost leader to buy low-cost supplies. Likewise, you'd expect businesses that differentiate on technology to value suppliers with innovative products. That also enables them to differentiate themselves.

Note: These three customer segment groups are generalizations. It's best to use customer survey techniques to determine your own customer segments and what they most value.

If you have only one offering at one price, for whom do you design the offering— the price buyer, relationship buyer, or technology buyer? And how do you price the offering? Do you price it very low to meet price buyers' needs or very high to capture the value that relationship or technology buyers are willing to pay for?

I most often observe offerings designed with all the bells and whistles to ensure they appeal to all groups but with a low price to capture the volume from all three groups—thus leaking a lot of value. Conversely, if the price is set high commensurate with the total value it brings, price buyers won't pay this price and volume will be lower. What to do?

Ideally, you would design two to three different offerings at various price points (gold, silver, bronze offerings) if you want to maximize your profits *and* volume. Segmenting and designing your differential offerings is often the easiest part of this journey. *Implementing* differential offerings, however, is not easy. I've seen many a great segmentation project shelved because they're so hard to implement. The biggest hurdle is the human factor; people in the organization might resist the change. Why?

- *It's difficult for your sales and technical service people to suddenly stop providing services to customers they've traditionally supplied. Their natural inclination is to give all the customers as much help as possible.*

- *Customer segmentation and policies also add a level of complexity. This makes the jobs of sales, customer service representatives, and technical personnel more difficult. They have more to remember—and often more than they can easily keep in their head.*

- *Your policies may not have taken into account the implications to the supply chain. Thus you may have the need to keep a large inventory or you risk encountering lower delivery-to-promise service. You may have even inadvertently reduced the amount of product your asset can produce due to the disruption of your asset scheduling caused by your policies. Any of these situations can cause friction among the commercial team and the supply chain/operation teams that will derail you.*

- *Your information systems might not easily enable a segmented offering approach or easily provide performance measures so you can track adherence to segmented policies.*

To be successful over the long haul, you'll need to put the following critical elements into place:

- *Your information system must be able to tag the customer to the segmented offering right through to:*
  - *the order desk (so the customer service rep only accepts orders within the policies for that customer);*
  - *the sales force (so prices are set and approved commensurate with the offering);*
  - *the service providers (so technical service and/or other service providers don't provide service to customers who aren't paying for that service); and*
  - *billing (so customers are appropriately charged).*

- *You need to have the following:*
  - *A tight, formal approval process for any deviations from policies and track adherence to these policies. Include these activities in your order fulfillment system.*
  - *Adherence metrics that are highly visible and ones that management acts upon when the policy adherence is not extremely high.*
  - *Clear expectations across your sales and technology teams regarding compliance to the offerings and policies.*
  - *Policies that take into consideration internal policies such as:*
    1) *demand prioritization (i.e., the policies that guide which market and customer segments will have higher priority for sales if you're limited in capacity) and*

2) *abnormal demand management (i.e., the policies that guide your order fulfillment actions if a customer orders higher volume shipments than normal monthly or expected shipments for delivery in the next month or so).*
   Without these, you will sub-optimize your profitability during tight sales/capacity times as well as underperform on your delivery-to-promise.

- *A way to maintain the discipline and courage to hold to your policies during tight and loose sales/capacity market conditions. Note: It's okay to modify policies for different supply/demand environments, but it's not good practice to ignore your policies when the market is loose. When the market sales/capacity is tight, you probably can't meet all of your customer order requests. Following your policies should result in accepting the customer orders that maximize your profits. During these times, the discipline of holding to your policies is generally quite clear and intuitive to the organization. However, when you have plenty of extra capacity, the organization may not see the need to follow your rules. They may view them as unnecessary bureaucracy and stop following them. On a number of occasions, I have seen this behavior create three unforeseen problems:*

1) *It creates confusion with customers, as they are unlikely to be able to predict when you will or will not follow your own policies;*

2) *It's difficult to turn "discipline" on and off. Or better said, it's easy to turn discipline off but difficult to restart it when the market turns tight again.*

3) *You can't always predict when you'll be limited in capacity and need to turn your discipline back on. An unexpected manufacturing or supply problem or an unexpected very large customer order can quickly throw you into a situation of not having enough product.*

- *Policies that align with your supply chain and resource capabilities. They need to be set with an understanding of the trade-off between profits, capacity, inventory, and delivery-to-promise. If they're not and your policies result in sub-optimizing the system, you'll have too much tension in the system and across functions to be successful. For example, if you set a two-day lead-time policy for your best customer segment group, but your supply chain has a natural replenishment time of one week, you risk failure. To meet the two days, the supply chain will need to increase inventory, risk missing the promised delivery date, or add additional product runs into the schedule, which can result in lost production. All these things go against the typical objectives of supply-chain managers.*

Holistic Value-Selling Approach

Holistic value selling includes the elements already listed, but it increases the sophistication with more customized value offers per customer. In addition, it involves a more sophisticated suite of tools to enable you to:

- *design the customized product and services,*

- *quantify and document the customer specific value,*

- *set the price,*

- *design the customized communication and negotiation package, and*

- *reward and recognize the value sellers in your sales force.*

Picture this. Jamie, one of your sales people, has identified a new customer. She quickly goes into your value-selling system and identifies both the typical value drivers for a customer in this market space and the value-based questions she will discuss with the customer. Through a conversation with the customer, Jamie gathers the information the system needs to fully quantify the expected monetary value for this customer. She then uses the prepared templates and guidance in the system to create:

1. two to three different product/service offerings at different price points that should meet the customer needs (and are in keeping with the allowable offerings approved by marketing);

2. the customer specific values of the offerings quantified, including the assumption and math that went into the quantifications;

3. a few relevant previously documented case histories to demonstrate or prove the company's value assertions; and

4. the professional-quality communication deck to take to the customer, which naturally and initially focuses discussions on value versus price.

Jamie is easily able to work with the customer to settle on the right value/price offering to meet both the customer's and your business needs.

Through the value discussions, Jamie identified a potential new product feature the customer would value and she brings this idea back to Brad, her marketing manager, and to the technology groups for consideration in future product design.

After the sale, Jamie will work with the customer to verify the benefits and value are achieved and then document this value in the system to expand the company's value-based case studies.

Jamie's compensation, which is based on delivering gross margin contribution and demonstrating she is a value seller (through the use of the value-selling tools) is high.

Refer to Play 5 on processes and systems; it discusses this more sophisticated approach in detail.

ADDITIONAL TIPS FOR NEGOTIATION AND VALUE-SELLING

NEGOTIATION

If you're having trouble convincing the customer of your value add and feel confident the customer would pay more for this value if the customer believed it was real—use creative techniques to lower the risks for the customer.

Examples of creative techniques include the following:

- Offer a trial price at no or little premium for the customer to test the product and verify the value.

- Offer a guarantee that the value will be at least X% better or you will rebate the difference between the premium and standard price.

- Consider a risk-sharing price mechanism. You get a base price plus a premium based on a share of the quantifiable benefits the customer receives.

- Offer the customer some price relief in exchange for rights to use the customer's data or name/quote/recommendation in your promotional information.

VALUE SELLING

- Value sellers need to consistently behave as value sellers to maintain credibility with the buyer. Buyers willing to pay more for a product have to believe you're pricing fairly for your value and fairly to them versus your other customers. No doubt buyers will likely test you as a way of determining the fairness of the offering. If they push you on price and you quickly cave, then you will have shown them you're not a value seller. This will encourage them to negotiate hard on price. Stand firm and committed to your value proposition.

- As a value seller, if a customer asks for a price concession, either take something away from the offering or gain something for the price concession. It must be apparent to customers that if they pay less, they get less, or they compensate you in a different way (such as share or volume gain or shifting to a product that delivers more margin for you). Takeaways can be things such as shorter payment terms, no technical service, freight not included, on-

line ordering only, or a number of other reduced features. Customers could also agree to
change their buying behaviors in a way that
financially benefits you, such as combining all
the orders into one monthly order or receiving
all their deliveries at one location rather than
multiple locations.

- Actions that undermine a value seller include
  offering discounts at the end of each quarter
  to pull sales forward or matching a competitor's price when you offer a higher value than
  that competitor offers.

- Marketing communications (i.e., brochures,
  industry journal articles, conference presentations, etc.) and customer-specific communication packages that clearly articulate your value
  are essential. The more proof you demonstrate
  with hard facts or customer case studies and
  the more your claims are stated in monetary
  terms, the more likely your customer base is
  to belief your claims. And customer perception of your claims is what it's all about.

After becoming familiar with how to analyze your transactional pricing and price leakage, let's move on to strategic
price setting. After all, every sports team needs a solid strategy to win the game!

Chapter 7:
Strategic Price Setting

One of the more powerful aspects of pricing is strategic price setting. I think of it as a process to set business strategy; it's a great way to refine your optimal business strategy by using the reality check of how much price or profit will realistically be generated under different strategies. It's my favorite part of pricing because of the challenge it offers and the high-gain benefits it can achieve.

Strategic pricing addresses industry-level, broad-based pricing dynamics and decisions. It involves carefully monitoring the industry and competitor dynamics to identify, predict, and/or influence favorable pricing dynamics.

In addition, it means quickly taking advantage of these dynamics. (Of course, it works in reverse, also; you can use these techniques to manage strategically through unfavorable market dynamics, such as market downturns.)

Lastly, when it's done well, the process includes looking at your multi-year future-potential pricing and market dynamics to set and revise your business strategy for greater long-term profitability.

Principles of Strategic Pricing

Strategic pricing is based on certain underlying assumptions or principles that include the following:

- *Competitors facing similar business or market dynamics (presuming they recognize these dynamics) have reason to act in similar ways.*

- *The actions of most mid- and large-size producers are likely to affect market dynamics, whether these actions are intentional or inadvertent.*

- *With proper, principled pricing leadership, your business can influence market pricing favorably.*

Now, if you can influence the market in a positive direction, it stands to reason you can influence it in a negative direction. And a negative direction often inadvertently occurs when you're not actively behaving in a disciplined, thoughtful manner. The more concentrated the competitive landscape, the more likely broad-based, disciplined behavior will emerge. As a rule of thumb, if at least half the market share is supplied from a handful of competitors, the dynamics have a higher potential to be favorable. The larger and more fragmented the market, though, the more difficult it is to successfully exert positive pricing pressure on the market price.

One of my more frustrating DuPont experiences occurred early in our pricing work when some leaders believed, "The market sets the price." This belief effectively shut down discussions on strategic pricing.

In effect, these leaders were implying that we were victims of the market. It took a while, but most of them eventually realized we can *choose* to be price leaders rather than *default* to being victims. With that shift, we were highly (but not always) successful. And without a doubt, when we were not actively trying to exert positive pricing pressure, we were inadvertently taking actions that hurt our price and the market price.

In the early years of my pricing work at DuPont, I often asked the business leaders which competitor(s) were driving price down. They never included themselves in the answer. But then I asked them how they thought their competitors would answer that question with respect to DuPont. At that point, many often admitted they had dropped price on occasion to gain share and might be viewed by our competitors as undisciplined and a contributor to lower market prices.

Another foundational underpinning of strategic pricing is that pricing over time (and presuming a loose sales/capacity ratio) will be set by the marginal producer—down to that producer's break-even cost and even down to this competitor's pricing at a variable cost level for short durations. Thus it's important to understand your competitor's cost to serve as well as the competitor's capacity.

Who is the marginal producer? The producer who is just barely able to eke out a profit at the current pricing and production levels. So the marginal producer will be a higher-cost producer but not necessarily the highest-cost producer. This producer can and does change with the sales/capacity ratio. Think of it this way. If the sales/capacity drops very low, the capacity of the highest-cost producers will not be needed in the market and these producers may stop producing; thus the marginal producer will be the next-highest-cost producer who continues to manufacture. Here's an example. Let's say the sales/capacity ratio is 50%—1,000 units of sales in a 2,000-unit capacity industry. Of four producers: Producer A and B have capacities of 400 units and costs of $1/unit; Producer C has a capacity of 500 units at $1.5/unit; and Producer D has a capacity of 700 units at $2/unit. It takes only the three producers with the lowest costs (Producers A, B, and C) to achieve a capacity of 1,000 units. Then the marginal producer becomes the highest-cost producer among these three, or Producer C, at $1.5/unit. The price could therefore fall to $1.5/unit. This example presumes that Producer D will stop producing product as the company is uncompetitive. Producer C will try to hold on for a while, at break-even cost, hoping the market will recover.

Here is one other very important point about strategic pricing: In some ways, strategic pricing is like a sports game, but in one crucial way, it's not at all. It's like a game in that you don't know what your opponent will do, so you try to predict the opponent's moves in reaction to your plays.

However, unlike a sports game, your objective with strategic pricing is not to beat the competitor but to create a win-win game, which might involve both opponents raising price, essentially increasing the market price. Why would you want a win-win game? Because over time, a win-lose game will almost always result in lower market prices and *both* you and your opponent will end up losing.

For example, if you raise your price but your opponent does *not,* perhaps in an attempt to intercept some of your market share, you may end up lowering your price to block the interception. Then the market price might end up lower than where it started—a lose-lose game.

But beware: Like a game, pricing has a referee—in this case, in the form of anti-trust laws that prevent you from colluding with your competitor.

The following sections provide guidance to raise the odds of creating a game that's win-win for all.

Favorable Market Dynamics

Let's explore favorable dynamics for *positive* pricing pressure or exerting leadership in the market.

Probably the two most obvious and commonly used levers are 1) shared pain and 2) tighter than average sales/capacity. Notice, I didn't say "tight sales/capacity." In fact, while tight is best, just being above the average or typical industry sales/capacity can be a favorable condition. Shared pain means most, if not all, competitors are facing similar pain. Shared pain can come in the form of rising raw material cost (something much of industry faced when oil prices started to rapidly elevate in 2005/2006). But it can also result from events such as rising costs affecting the industry at large—possibly from new regulation requirements or rising freight charges. Another form of shared pain might be persistent low-to-negative profitability across the industry.

Market breaks might also be a favorable pricing lever. For example, a few years ago, broad concerns were raised in the U.S. over the safety of toys made in China. Whether this concern was real or misperceived is immaterial. It likely presented the opportunity for U.S. toy companies to raise prices versus China's toy prices.

Yet another favorable pricing dynamic is competitors raising price. If your competitors raise prices, odds are you can successfully raise prices, too.

The likelihood of taking advantage of favorable pricing dynamics, or at least of being a first mover in price increases, goes up if your company:

- *is one of a handful of large players that have at least half the market share,*

- *makes pricing moves that are fairly apparent and visible to the marketplace, and*

- *doesn't face a large, significantly cost-advantaged player (unless it is you).*

With fewer players, it's often (but not always) easier to gather competitive intelligence, guess or predict competitors' actions, and feel the direct impact of competitors' actions—just as competitors are able to do with you. Depending on the discipline of the market, this can work *for* you or *against* you. That's why it's important to set strategies that maximize the odds of it working *for* you—never an easy task, but often a doable one.

> # BY THE WAY . . .
>
> Your company doesn't need to be the largest supplier to be the first to make price moves. Being one of the top value leaders in your industry is ideal for making your company a price leader.

Market Messaging

Market messaging is a critical element of strategic pricing, as you need to have a degree of transparency to your actions. Although I provide some guidance here, *you absolutely must get legal counsel in this area* to ensure you're congruent with the laws in your region.

It probably goes without saying, but I will say it anyway: *Never, never talk to your competitors about pricing.* Strategic pricing is not, and never should be, about colluding with competitors to set price. Your messaging must focus on what *you* are experiencing and what *you* are doing, and it should be directed to your market/customer base.

Avenues for Your Message

You can get your message out to the market via a number of avenues, and using several of them is ideal. Consider:

- *price letters to customers,*

- *pricing lists and/or messages on your website,*

- *letters or training for your distributors,*

- *customer visits/discussions to set the stage, and*

- *articles on industry health or trade journal interviews.*

Don't forget to fully train and communicate your key messages internally to your sales force, CSRs, and commercial leadership. They must understand and believe in the pricing rationale so they can credibly communicate price to customers. Make sure your internal team knows you have a fair and credible reason for your pricing moves, just as you do with your customers. Your goal? For your customers to feel fairly treated and trust you.

What Belongs in Your Market Message?

Share your views of the relative industry dynamics, the impact to you, and thus your rationale for making price moves. This is also an ideal time to stress your strong commitment to the market and discuss any specific value you bring to the market, especially newly added value (e.g., investing in new products or supply expansions). In avenues such as customer letters, you can also include pricing or sales policy specifics.

For your larger customers, tailor your customer letters to include specific value-added services you've recently supplied to the customer (e.g., technical service on X situation, new product development for their specific needs, training courses).

SAMPLE LETTER TO YOUR CUSTOMERS

Dear Customer,

I'm writing to express our appreciation for your business and your loyalty. I also would like to provide you with some background on the price increase we're in the process of implementing. Over the past few years, the unprecedented rise in energy costs and most of the key raw materials used to make industrial and chemical products have taken a heavy toll on the profitability of our business. Our raw materials have increased over 20% in the past two years alone.

We continue to diligently work on lowering our internal costs in a way that doesn't hamper our ability to bring the innovative solutions our customers expect from us. The squeeze in our profit margins makes it increasingly difficult to manage this balance.

I am ready and willing to discuss these and other issues with you in the spirit of partnership and mutual benefits. Again, thank you for your business and loyalty.

Sincerely,

Disciplined Behaviors

Once you've set and communicated your price increase, ensure that you:

- *are fair and trustworthy,*

- *are predictable,*

- *consistently and unwaveringly do what you say you will do, and*

- *react quickly and thoughtfully to competitive threats.*

If you consistently operate with disciplined behaviors, it will result in positive pricing pressure on the market. Webster's dictionary describes discipline as "orderly or prescribed conduct or pattern of behavior." For pricing effectiveness, I like to think of these patterns of behavior as honorable, courteous behaviors.

Note: These four actions work together. For example, you will not be viewed as trustworthy if you're unpredictable or take actions that differ from your words. The more your customers trust you and can predict your actions, the more accepting they will be of your price moves. Likewise, the more your competitors think they can predict your actions and believe you won't use price drops as a means to buy share, the more likely they are to avoid pricing behaviors that create negative pricing pressure on the industry.

For customers to view you as fair and trustworthy, they must believe your price increase rationale is credible and appropriate. They also must believe that similar customers will also be hit with the same price moves. *You will absolutely undermine your hard work if you don't follow through with what you said you would do.* At the same time, be willing to walk away from some volume.

Note: Again, if the volume decline appears to be higher than expected or desired given the price/volume break-even point, then you'll have to regroup. But I have yet to see that necessity with businesses that followed sound strategic pricing practices.

If your competitors attempt to use this situation to go after your loyal customers with lower prices, act quickly and decisively to dissuade this play. You can discourage it by rapidly going after one of their loyal customers with a similar approach to the one they used. For example, if they offered your customer a 5% discount, then within 24 hours, you offer a 5% discount to one of their loyal customers. Make that point only once; then go back to purposeful and disciplined behavior.

What will happen? Those competitors will likely get the message and know you won't stand idly by while they cherry-pick your customers. Consider this: If you hold a grudge and continue to punish a competitor, your competitor will have little choice but to continue the disruptive behavior. What happens? In the end, you will both lose.

Lastly, be disciplined and purposeful both during and after the price increase. By disciplined, I mean consistently take actions that support higher industry prices. Do not drop price to gain share. This undisciplined behavior will have a negative impact on market prices and quite often won't result in share gain. The more consistently you follow disciplined behaviors through a few price increase cycles, the more successful you're likely to be. In the long run, you gain the trust and predictability you need.

I remember a DuPont case in which one of our competitors went to one of our largest loyal customers with a very low price. In fact, we believed the price to be lower than this competitor was offering its own loyal customers. As often happens in these situations, our customer called asking us to match this low price. Within a day, we contacted one of the large loyal customers of the competitor. We offered that company a similarly low price. We indicated we knew the customer likely had already been offered pricing this low, given its primary supplier appeared to be offering low prices in the marketplace, but we felt we had more value to offer.

Lo and behold, within the next 24 hours, this competitor had pulled back its low-ball price offer to our loyal customer—and the games stopped. We retained our customer at the higher price rate.

We could only speculate, of course, but we assumed the competitor's loyal customer went back to the supplier, insisting on also getting the low price the supplier was offering others. No doubt this loyal customer wanted to know why the supplier hadn't equally offered this price break. The competitor had lost the trust of its large loyal customer and was then in damage-control mode.

That's how to lose the pricing game!

Multi-Year Strategic Pricing

Strategic pricing is not limited to broad-based short-term price increases. It can be so much more powerful when you analyze and predict a multi-year time horizon and then use these insights to refine your strategy for enhanced future profitability. I think of this as a profit-back business strategy.

As noted earlier, your project team consists of experts from the central group such as the senior pricing manager, one or two analysts, and a competitive intelligence expert, if you have one. On the business side, the leader is often a product-line manager accompanied by others such as a pricing or financial analyst and possibly a competitive intelligence leader from the business (if one exists). Of course, as with all pricing projects, you'll include others from the commercial team as needed. The business leader's input will be important throughout the project due to the high potential for this type project to impact the business strategy or have broad-reaching implications to the business.

The team is charged with analyzing foundational data for a few years of history as well as projecting it at least three years into the future. These historical analyses and predictions include the standard analyses you would do when setting your business strategy plus a few more:

- *Competitive costs and capacity*

- *Key raw material trends*

- *Market size and growth rate*

- *Industry sales/capacity*

- *Pricing history and historical pricing mechanisms*

- *Competitor SWOT analysis (Strengths, Weaknesses, Opportunities, Threats)*

- *Industry trends in profitability, costs, regulations, market needs, etc.*

- *Customer/market/region profitability*

With this foundation, you should be able to predict the market sales/capacity as well as pricing and market profitability, and thus predict the profitability of your business.

As you analyze the historical pricing mechanisms, can you see a correlation between the supply/demand and your industry prices? During loose sales/capacity times, can you correlate the industry price to the total or variable cost of the marginal cost producer? As the market tightens, the price should increase toward value-based pricing. Can you identify the historical pricing pattern? You can see potential swings in pricing dynamics for the coming years, and you have the time to influence the future to your advantage.

Business Strategy Levers

Consider the many levers available to improve your short, mid-, and long-term profitability by either influencing market dynamics or positioning your business to take advantage of market dynamics. Some possible levers include the following:

- **Supply changes:** *Consider changes that might permanently or temporarily tighten supply and demand, such as: swap/co-producer sales agreements, switching of raw material sources, inventory builds or reductions, maintenance/shutdown timing, export strategy.*

- **Asset changes:** *Consider factors that might permanently or temporarily tighten the market or improve your profits and/or capacity, such as shutdown of idle facilities, shutdown of high-cost facilities, asset optimization studies, capacity expansions or consolidations, lean manufacturing, acquisition of capacity.*

- **Business model(s) and practices:** *Think about such changes as: market channel/distribution or value chain changes, sales or technical service and development changes, differential management of commodity versus specialty portions of the business, product portfolio changes, pricing process and practices enhancements, product/service price bundling.*

- **Differentiation:** *Make changes to create higher value and higher prices, for example, through these factors: product or application innovation, establishing a fighter brand (i.e., a low-cost, low-value offering targeted at customers who buy predominately on price alone), enhanced service (e.g., responsiveness, reliability, lead-time), customer education for value understanding.*

- **Sales contract management:** *Modify your sales contracts, potentially taking different approaches during tight-demand/supply timeframes versus weak-demand/supply timeframes. This might mean: a) shifting toward a spot market (i.e., no agreements; every order is based on the price you set that day) during tight markets; or b) shifting toward locking in customers with contracts just before a predicted period of loose market conditions. Modify price formulas (e.g., cost plus—your price escalated with a given raw material, index based, meaning your price changes relative to a specific publically available index such as Chemical Producer Index, etc.). Change risk-based terms (e.g., contract duration, min/max volume, etc.) and sales policies.*

- **Targeting and differential pricing:** *Consider changes to your market priorities. For example, target attractive regions, markets, applications, customers, product breadth and mix, given your market dynamic predictions.*

- **Consistent messaging:** *Use market messaging to influence behaviors. Consider price releases, industry associations, newsletters, field behavior, etc. Discuss your views or plans on situations such as capacity expansions or consolidations, major annual shutdowns, market trends, and so on.*

Strategies Used at DuPont

Early in my career as a business manager, I successfully used the principles of strategy pricing to turn around the profitability of various businesses. At the time, however, I had never heard of strategic pricing. In effect, I was creating my approach as I went along. Let me share one example.

I was given a by-product business to manage that suffered from negative earnings. The by-product came from a seasonal core product, thus we had high amounts of the by-product during the main season and very limited amounts off season. Unfortunately for DuPont, the market wanted and needed a flat supply throughout the year. We had limited storage, so during the heavy season for the core product, we had far more by-product than we could sell, even when we dropped the price substantially (which we routinely had to do). With limited storage, we ended up disposing of the excess as waste. During the off season, we didn't have sufficient product and thus were viewed as unreliable. This behavior was severely hurting our ability to capture a fair market price. Further, we were disruptive to the overall market, creating constant cycles of tight and loose market conditions as well as depressing market price.

At the time, we were keenly motivated by environmental responsibility to eliminate any waste. So I reasoned that the best way to eliminate waste was to become a reliable supplier. That meant we needed to have consistent supply throughout the year. Therefore, we created a low-cost swap arrangement with another producer, one who intentionally produced and thus did not face the seasonality challenge that we faced. For a nominal fee, they took some of our excess product in our heavy season and returned the product in our light season. We also increased our storage capability and brought on a new distributor to expand our market reach. These actions allowed us to flatten our supply. Thus, as a reliable supplier, we were able to command higher prices. Our changed behavior stopped causing the cyclical market dynamics of tight supply, loose supply. As a result, our customers were better served and overall market prices increased. Nothing like getting a touchdown and making the extra point, too!

In DuPont, we successfully performed dozens of strategic pricing projects and incorporated disciplined behaviors into our businesses. In the early years of our pricing efforts, on two occasions we used the McKinsey consulting firm to lead or partner with us in executing strategy pricing projects.

All the planning and strategy in the world won't win the game if your execution is poor. Play 4 addresses elements of execution that are key to your success.

PLAY 4:
THE RIGHT EXECUTION

It's time for the big game. You have the right team and the right plays; you're set up for success. However, winning ultimately comes down to how well you execute your plays. It's the same in pricing.

A good strategy without good execution won't win you profits. In fact, the inability to execute price strategy well was a key failure for many DuPont businesses before we began our efforts to enhance our pricing competency.

While increasing price or introducing pricing on new products are the predominate skills needed, you must also excel at decreasing price or matching a lower competitive offer. With the world macroeconomic conditions, along with changing market needs and increasing global competition, you will almost certainly need to work price in both directions. You must be strong at offensive moves plus defensive moves, not to mention special team plays.

The next two chapters cover how to execute price increases and how to execute price decreases to maximize your effectiveness.

Chapter 8:
Price Increase Effectiveness

Even if you're good at setting price, you can still be unsuccessful when it comes to implementing the price.

Yes, even if you're raising the price to a fair value-in-use position, you have no guarantee of success. Let's face it, raising price is no fun, and it can even be unnerving. After all, it's quite likely your business has share and/or volume growth targets to meet. If you raise price too high, you risk losing volume. If your sales people tell you they tried to raise price in the past but were unsuccessful, what should you conclude? Either they set the price too high or your sales force didn't have the organizational ability to be effective.

In my experience, failure to successfully implement a price increase is quite common—and the underlying cause is often lack of effective price execution more than overpriced products.

After watching hundreds of pricing increases—some successful, others not so much—I've noticed consistent trends that reveal 10 key elements necessary for success. While all 10 are important, the first three appear to be the most critical for success.

1. **Leadership:** Pricing is a highly visible top priority, with urgency for top management. Aggressive targets and unwavering high expectations are set. Leaders proactively instill confidence in the organization's ability to accomplish the increase. And they explicitly own the risk of lost volume, thus minimizing the burden on the sales force. In fact, leaders must be expecting and willing to

lose a little volume. If they're not, they won't have the backbone needed to hold their ground. Yes, this can be a game of chicken, and the one who blinks first often loses. Of course, leaders also want to be smart about where they're willing to take the volume loss (as discussed in previous chapters). Lastly, marketing and sales leadership, as well as global and regional leadership, succeed when they act as one aligned team. That requires creating a steering team that meets regularly to set and guide the pricing strategy and guidance.

2. **Resource for success:** One person (e.g., a pricing manager who has sufficient time and delegated priority) is made accountable for coordinating and guiding the organization through the price-increase implementation as well as closely tracking progress and raising a flag if you are not meeting either your pricing or your timing targets. This person may be the facilitator but not necessarily the decision maker.

3. **Customer relations:** Significant effort is given to building and/or sustaining customer relationships throughout the price increase and after. One successful DuPont sales director was fond of saying, "We might lose the volume, but we will not lose the customer." It's critical that customers believe they're being (and actually are being) treated fairly, respectfully, and honestly. The most successful sales forces have a deep understanding of their customers' buying/decision-making processes and needs as well as the impact of the price increase. They proactively support their customers in either "selling" the increase to their managers and/or passing the increase along

to their customers. It's critical they stay closely connected to the customer after the increase to provide support and learn about any difficulties.

4. **Communication:** Communication, both internally to your organization and externally to the customer base, is also critical. Internal communications should be prepared, predominately for the sales and customer service representatives, but also for anyone who interfaces with customers. This communication includes an in-depth rationale for the increase as well as market and competitive dynamics, business risks, value-in-use quantification, external communication packages, and frequently asked questions and answers.

   External communications will be a stripped-down version of internal communications. (See Play 3: Chapter 7 for guidance on strategic pricing messaging.) The external communications are often tailored for different market or customer segments, highlighting various value-in-use messages or different market dynamics. For strategic accounts, you may even develop customized communications by adding customer-specific information about their specific buying behaviors or the extra services/value you have recently provided for them.

   Note: The pricing manager or marketing manager takes on the responsibility of drafting these communications (often with the help of your marketing communication resources) and working with the sales leaders to implement them.

This is just the beginning. The communication process continues throughout the implementation. The most successful organizations make other efforts, such as weekly sales force conference calls to share wins, build confidence, and share competitive learnings.

5. **Disciplined processes:** Pricing targets have to be set at a granular level (i.e., by customer/product/salesperson) followed by agreed-upon targets by the sales person and his or her manager. Risk guidance related to your risk volume-loss tolerance is provided at a granular level (i.e., by segment, product family, and/or margin) so the sales force knows where to stand firm and where to back off.

Advice: Test your market first with the segments in which you're most willing to risk volume loss. This will give you more confidence as you approach more valuable segments. Putting contingency plans in place is also a good practice.

Use a single performance tracking database or system that extends to the granular level. Remember, the credibility of your data is key. Your organization must have trust in the customer/product profitability data (e.g., price, margin, real variable or fixed costs, etc.) to feel confident that you've set appropriate price-increase targets. Therefore, be sure your underlying customer and product profitability data are routinely updated and credible.

It helps to have standard contracts or standard written agreements for all customer agreements. These should contain standard price opener clauses (ideally 30 days for many markets) and standard payment terms. If the nature of your business warrants volume price brackets, rebates, minimum volume buys, and so on, then be sure these are clearly stated. Also be sure your contract tracking system allows you to easily monitor performance against these conditions. Part of the process consists of continual monitoring of the market and competitive dynamics.

6. **Metrics:** Weekly tracking of price-increase implementation progress is handled at the customer/product/sales person level. Be sure business volume losses are tracked, including who, how much, and under what conditions.

7. **Recognition and rewards:** It's important to recognize strong performers and celebrate "wins" (i.e., successful negotiations, especially those early in the implementation). For example, you'd highlight these in your weekly sales force meeting or send a monthly email that conveys the early or significant wins.

   Sales compensation is another contributing factor. If your sales force is on variable pay and a majority factor in compensation is price or margin gain, this will enhance your success. On the other hand, compensation metrics that predominately reward volume will work against you.

8. **Training and coaching:** Providing training and coaching on price pressure negotiation skills, including how to respond when competitors offer lower prices, improves success.

9. **Negotiation practices:** If conceding a price target with a customer, the sales person routinely gets

some customer concession in return (e.g., reduced service, more share, etc.). Some customer price increases, or elements of the increase, are not negotiable (as set by the leadership). The customer accepts the offer or you walk away. To test the market and gain confidence, price increases are first negotiated at the lowest profitable strategic segments or customers. New prices go into effect on the targeted date even if negotiations are not yet finalized (i.e., the interim price during negotiations is the target price).

10. **Speed and urgency:** It's important to understand the time cycles: first, recognizing the need to increase price (or when you should have identified the need); the time to announce the increase; the negotiation time window; and, finally, the time the price goes into effect. I've seen many businesses take three or more months to successfully achieve their desired increases, while others have taken closer to one month. Once you experience an implementation cycle time, improve it. Look for the key time barriers—such as slow decision making, contracts with no price openers, or slowly generated communication packages—then find solutions to improve the performance.

At the end of the day, your financial returns are a function of the amount of increase you achieved and the speed at which you begin to realize the benefits. It's like the fourth quarter of the football game with two minutes to go and your team needs a touchdown to win. You must make that touchdown *plus* do it within a short timeframe; so be sure to focus on both.

Chapter 9:
Price Decrease Effectiveness

You hate to do it, but at times, the smartest move you can make is to drop price. These times are often associated with major market softening, low demand/supply ratios, or your offering's value to the customer declining relative to competitive products. You are now on the defensive team. A skilled pricing organization must be capable of decreasing price effectively as well as increasing it effectively. But there's good news. The principles that underpin strategic and value pricing hold whether you're increasing *or* decreasing price. You just follow them in reverse. Your three main goals are to:

- *reduce your price only as low as necessary,*

- *gain some concession or value for giving up price, and*

- *delay the price reduction as long as you can do so appropriately.*

The following checklist and guidance will help you manage all three.

Checklist of Favorable Conditions for Dropping Price

When considering a price drop, it will help to answer the following questions. If your answers are all "favorable," then move forward with the decrease. However, if any of the answers are "unfavorable," rethink the need to drop your price.

Why are you considering a drop?

Favorable: Competitors are lowering prices or to stimulate increased market demand.

Unfavorable: To meet customer desire/expectation; to gain share; to pull sales forward into next financial quarter/year

What will happen if you don't drop price?

Favorable: Potential loss of a large share of desirable customers

Unfavorable: No or minimal share loss

How likely is share loss?

Favorable: Highly likely to lose share

Unfavorable: Unlikely; product re-qualifications would be needed; downstream customers are pulling for you.

To whom will you lose the share?

Favorable: One of the top suppliers

Unfavorable: A new (un-established), small, or low-end competitor; an opportunistic importer

What is the customer's traditional behavior?

Favorable: Not loyal; switch suppliers often; a price buyer

Unfavorable: Loyal; value buyer

Are customer needs changing? Is your value proposition clear?

Favorable: Competitors are closing the gap; the customer no longer needs your value.

Unfavorable: Your value is clear and the customer needs this value.

What product grades are at risk for share loss? Are you only targeting the at-risk grades?

Favorable: Only ABC grades or commodity grades are at risk and you're targeting only these for price drop.

Unfavorable: Grades DCF or unique/custom grades are not at risk but have been included in the price drop.

What is the account variable margin?

Favorable: High or higher than similar customers

Unfavorable: Low or lower than similar customers

What is the break-even volume?

Favorable: The volume gain (if there is one) will more than offset the price contribution loss; or the volume saved (presuming you would have lost volume) more than offsets the price-contribution loss of this segment. Overall variable contribution dollars increase.

Unfavorable: Volume gain will not offset the price/margin decline. Total profitability will decline.

What is the competitive offering, including value, terms, volume, etc. compared to your offering?

Favorable: Comparable to yours. Competitor is a large, reliable supplier with a sustainable offer.

Unfavorable: Lower value offering. Competitor is an untried or potentially unreliable supplier. Competitor is only offering a one-time buy or a short-term offer.

Have you gotten past the buyer to sell your value?

Favorable: Reached out to the business beyond buyer with little impact. They don't appreciate your value relative to your price.

Unfavorable: Commercial team sees your value and does not want to shift away. Downstream customer pull exists.

If in response to a competitor offering lower prices to your accounts, have you tried to counter the competitor's price cuts?

Favorable: You offered the same low price to the competitor's customers. Competitor continues with price cuts.

Unfavorable: You offered the same low price to the competitor's customers. The competitor is not continuing to cut prices.

Do you have a solid rationale for holding/increasing price? How did you justify increases in the past?

Favorable: No solid rationale for holding/increasing price. Past increases were done on the basis of your rising raw material costs. Raw material prices are now dropping and you've recovered your margin. Or, the customer volume is increasing significantly.

Unfavorable: Yes, you have a solid rationale for holding/ increasing price. Customer is below average on profitability. Customer volume is dropping. Your raw material costs are increasing. Your offering has higher value than that of competitors.

Will there be competitive reaction or spillover to other customers?

Favorable: Competitors and other customers are unlikely to know of your price drop, so no spillover effect is expected. Competitors are unlikely to drop price.

Unfavorable: Your price drop is likely visible to competitors and other customers. Spillover could be expected. Competitors will probably react with even further price drops.

Guidance on How to Effectively Drop Price

If you've determined that dropping price is necessary, then consider the suggestions in this list to minimize the decrease, make it more successful, and/or improve the timing.

1. Calculate your value over competition to set the appropriate price premium.

    *   *Consider all elements of product, service, brand, and relationship value.*

    *   *Is the customer's downstream price or growth higher with your products?*

- *Are the customer's production costs, capacity, and/or quality improved with your products?*

- *Consider factors such as cost and/or perceived risk of switching, innovation, reliability, and trust.*

- *Get all the details of the competitive offer you're being asked to match (volume, terms, package/order size, origin of material, etc.). When customers ask you to match a competitive offer, they should be willing to supply these details. If they won't, be suspicious.*

2. Would adding more value to your offering help you hold price?

- *Examples: Extension of warranties or guarantees, shorter lead times, co-branding, six-month exclusivity on new products, credit, training sessions*

3. Demonstrate that you're a value pricer by taking something away when you drop price.

- *Examples: Longer lead times, shorter payment terms, longer contract commitment, no custom products, no technical service, freight excluded, weekday delivery only*

4. For your most attractive customers, have you considered asking for customer concessions versus takeaways?

- *Examples: More share, longer contract commitment, first right for future applications, access to performance data on your products versus competitive products, access to decision makers*

5. Consider using temporary discounts.

   - *Examples: Temporary 90-day discount or rebate, 60-day trial period at X% discount*

6. Consider offering two or three choices (low value/low price, high value/high price) to stimulate value discussions and better meet customer needs. Examples:

   - *Low value/low price: Core products only, six-weeks delivery, full truckload and no service*

   - *Mid value/mid price: Most products, one-week lead time, technical service*

   - *High value/high price: All products, two-day lead time, net/45 payment terms, 24-hour technical service hotline*

7. Keep a slight premium over an alternative supplier when you're the incumbent supplier. Examples:

   - *Minimum 2-3% higher than an alternate supplier of like reputation*

   - *Minimum 5% higher for less established supplier*

8. Consider reducing price only on the customer's last increment of business. Examples:

   - *First 100 tons at $2/ton and next 10 tons at $1.90/ton*

- *Rebate only on portion of product that customer sells through to low-value applications*

- *Use cumulative volume rebates*

9. Remove volume discounts/rebates if customer volume drops.

  - *Example: Shift from something like 5% discount from list price to 5% rebate if purchases hit a quarterly minimum of X.*

10. Run the economics to understand impact to earnings/contribution.

  - *New contribution: (New Price - Variable Cost) x New Volume*

  - *Old contribution: (Current Price - Variable Cost) x Expected Volume*

11. Be consistent with your preset pricing policies and plans versus one-off decisions. You may need to modify policies.

  - *Example: Products XYZ price drop up to X%; hold price on products ABC; defend accounts with margin over 40%.*

12. Reduce price only on your specific at-risk products.

  - *Examples: 5% on commodity grades ABC; 0% on unique grades DEF*

13. Encourage customers to switch to a product that's more attractive to you (higher margin, core product). Examples:

- *Products A and B are both priced at $2/kg, but product B has 10% higher variable margin. Lower product B price slightly and shift customer from product A to B.*

- *Shift away from custom/very low volume products*

14. Use stall tactics to drag out the negotiation.

- *Examples: Negotiate over several meetings (first to understand their needs, next to present choices, separate meeting with your boss . . .); require director approval.*

I often see businesses take many months to implement price increases after favorable market dynamics are apparent (for example, their raw materials go up 10% and they take months to pass it along). Then, when market conditions turn unfavorable, they're much quicker to drop the price (for example, their raw materials drop 10% and they pass the savings along within one month). At a minimum, if possible, don't reduce prices any faster than you increase prices. Furthermore, don't assume it's a given that you must give all of the price back—especially, if you've been losing margin for years. Evaluate the situation, and if you have a credible, fair rationale for holding or only dropping slightly, then act on this rationale.

Keep in mind that market messaging and communications with the customer base in times of price increase (as described in the strategic pricing chapter) still hold in times of price decrease. Keep the lines of communication open. Consider the situation in which most competitors are likely to drop price, perhaps due to a large raw material price drop. You're often better off to communicate your pricing position first; be a price leader in the decline of price. For example, you might communicate that you intend to drop prices in the following quarter by 5%. That proactive step may prevent market pressures from building toward a larger and faster drop, say a 10% drop in the current month.

Play 5 discusses the systems you'll need to support and facilitate your pricing efforts.

PLAY 5:
THE RIGHT SYSTEMS

Look at any successful football teams and you're sure to find they have invested in the latest and greatest technology (e.g., for training, injury/rehabilitation, video replaying, communication headsets, equipment, etc.). They also monitor performance statistics and incorporate other disciplined processes (e.g., pre-season training, pre-game preparation, post-game evaluations, talent scouting....).

Likewise, to be successful, pricing requires effective, disciplined processes and systems as well as credible data. You may not need all these from day one, but you will eventually. This play discusses each of these processes and its system implications.

The three internal pricing management processes plus performance management process are best handled thoughtfully and holistically in one common information system. Here's what they involve:

Price setting: setting and refreshing optimal prices—by market segment, customer segment, and customer—based on solid transactional, value, and strategic pricing analyses

Customer deal management: managing the specific customer price and terms negotiations relative to your pricing targets and policies so you can execute more profitable deals

Price administration: administering price and policies—from list price to customer offer to invoice—in an accurate and timely manner

Performance management and analytics: analyzing and tracking your performance to identify opportunities to improve profit margins and enhance compliance to price targets and policies

Value selling: In addition, a core external value-selling pricing process deserves careful thought, attention, and an enabling system(s) that includes: a) understanding your customer needs and tailoring your offering toward meeting those needs; b) quantifying the value for the customer or market segment; and c) communicating the value to the customer in a way that creates customer confidence, trust, and buy-in. This enhances your ability to capture your fair value.

If you're early in your pricing maturity, robust systems are likely to be of lesser importance; you can make do with spreadsheets. But if you aspire to world-class (or even slightly better than mediocre) performance, be thinking about investing in systems to sustainably and effectively help you achieve optimal prices with speed. Remember, the core internal processes are tightly linked; ideally, you'd manage them in one holistic system.

Price and Profitability Analytics

Analytics form the backbone of your decisions and performance management. The stronger your systems are in providing quick, accurate, and insightful analysis, the better and faster you'll be with pricing decisions. Without good systems, your pricing and commercial teams could spend (or waste) significant time gathering data and generating analysis rather than getting on with the insights and actions that drive profits.

Advice: If you find it very difficult to obtain data and analysis, you're unlikely to sustain the process.

Face it. Pricing analytics aren't a sometime thing. (That might be a great way to start your pricing transformation, but it's not an end point.) As you progress in your pricing maturity, you'll move to monthly refreshes, and as you reach world class, the standard becomes real-time data and dashboards (i.e., 24-hour refresh) at a highly granular level (i.e., by segment, customer, sales person, territory, product) that are readily available to your marketing, pricing, and sales teams. To get a picture of world class, think of the real-time, extensive football team and player performance statistics available—not just to the coaches but on the Internet.

Initially, you can accomplish your analysis in Excel or Access databases. But be aware that you can significantly increase the speed and quality of your analysis with low-cost analytics software (such as Tableau), which can be licensed for your pricing analysts or pricing managers. This software can take weeks off a project timeline, while allowing you to test numerous hypotheses regarding pricing leakage and opportunities.

Analytic systems you might consider (in order of increasing investment) include:

- *Excel or Access with Tableau Software (www. TableauSoftware.com) or other analytic software licenses*

- *Homegrown analytic systems with manual refresh*

- *Homegrown analytic systems with automatic refresh*

- *Commercially available analytic systems (Vendavo – www.vendavo.com, Analytics Pros – www.pros.com, etc.)*

If you aspire to be a world-class pricer, I suggest investing in a holistic, commercially available pricing system such as Vendavo that includes analytics but extends into a full closed-loop system with the critical internal pricing processes. However, a word of caution: I've watched a few companies, including DuPont, begin to invest in these full systems only to stop implementation or severely limit their use to the analytics capability (more about this later).

Analytics are critical, but they're likely to bring in only 20% of the value of a holistic system. That makes these holistic systems quite expensive if you don't plan to use their value-added modules. If you want only analytics, I recommend using one of the less expensive system options listed above and linking it with a software tool such as Tableau. For DuPont, Tableau made a night-and-day difference in our analytics effectiveness. It was both affordable and easy to learn for pricing practitioners.

Price Setting Systems

If your objective is to optimize your profits, you'll need to set price targets, guidance, and policies at a highly granular level. Not only is it wise to think about the price of each product and product package, you need to think about adjustments/discounts for market segments, customer segments, regional segments, and different-sized accounts or volume brackets. Other price considerations might include agreement terms and conditions such as payment terms, minimum order quantities, lead times, services, and surcharges for special requests.

To do this well, rely on strong analytics to assess your historical trends, your variance at a granular level, and your compliance to your pricing targets and policies. Ideally, including your price setting in the same system as your analytics and performance management will facilitate faster, smarter decisions.

Price Administration Systems

Price administration works hand in hand with price setting. Once you set prices, you have to administer them to the sales force, customer service representatives, and your order-to-cash systems (i.e., your systems for taking orders and billing customers). If your price setting and administration are integrated in the same system, then you can implement price changes more quickly and accurately.

Advice: Investing in a good system can make the difference of several weeks in implementing your price increases for complex product lines. That is *real* money!

Deal Negotiation Support Systems

The sales force has the tough role of negotiating the best deal with each customer. Ideally, each sales person would negotiate to list price and fully align with your sales policies. But in the real world, at least in B2B markets, that often doesn't happen. Thus the sales person needs guidance and approval regarding any deviations from your standard list price and offering.

Naturally, the customer wants fast decisions on the price proposal, but it can be quite time consuming for the sales person to get the deal approved by his or her manager. So when faced with an off-list price deal, the manager has to understand the profit implications of the deal as it compares to similar deals and the price list before making a thoughtful decision. Once a deal is approved, it must be documented and then put into the order-to-cash system. Without good intelligent systems, value can leak through the line in plenty of places. For example:

- *Sales people and CSRs taking orders against old prices versus new price lists*

- *Billing the customer using the old price versus the new price*

- *Negotiating a deal below price guidance or below your typical deals*

- *Approving deals with little idea of how they stack up against similar deals*

- *Defaulting to average pricing versus segmented pricing*

- *Losing time getting approval by the right level of management*

- *Losing sales due to a slow approval process*

- *By-passing the appropriate approval levels to make deals*

When your price negotiation system is tied to your price-setting and administration system and to your price analytics, these problems are minimized, and once again, you'll make smarter, faster decisions.

Performance Management System

You need to track your actual performance, win/loss rates, and adherence to pricing guidance and policies to:

- *ensure you're executing well,*

- *test if your guidance and policies are actually delivering the expected profits,*

- *investigate root causes of pricing variability,*

- *establish segmentation hypotheses, and*

- *repeat the process, setting the next level of pricing moves.*

So here's the broken record: *If your performance management system is integrated with your deal negotiation and price administration systems, you can assess performance more quickly than ever.*

Closed-Loop System

When your pricing systems are integrated in a closed-loop manner, you significantly improve your pricing optimization and do so with much less effort. Although it's quite an investment to put in a closed-loop process, the rewards are also great.

While going this route appears to be the best option for pricing effectiveness, it does require a significant amount of investment, change management, process optimization design, commitment from leadership, and potentially a multi-year journey to fully implement. So proceed carefully. I've seen a number of companies complete this full journey and others (such as DuPont) stop the journey part way. Often recessions, down markets, or management changes create this challenge to staying the course.

If it were my own company and my sole decision (presuming a diverse, complex business), I wouldn't hesitate to invest in a topnotch commercial pricing system.

Data Quality

No matter what systems you choose to use, data quality must be high and credible within the organization. This can take significant work in itself and is not to be underestimated. As discussed in Play 3: Chapter 5 on transactional pricing, look out for these pitfalls:

- *Variable costs that aren't properly assigned to the individual product*

- *Fixed costs that are allocated and thus not properly assigned to the individual product*

- *Freight charges that are allocated*

- *Payment terms, early payment discounts, contract volume requirements, rebates, discounts, contract length, segmentation tagging, etc., that may be found in disparate data systems or files*

You'll have to make a judgment call as to which of your data streams are important and feasible enough to cleanse. Variable costs are almost always worth cleansing and analyzing. All others may or may not be.

For example, if freight costs are a small portion of your total cost, and it would be difficult to get them properly assigned into your system, then you might opt to not do this task. Likewise, fixed cost (as discussed earlier) is not a key component of your ongoing short-term price/volume decisions. While freight and fixed costs would be nice to have, they're not a must.

Value-Selling and Value Communications

If you aspire to be a value merchant, you'll need the processes, tools, and systems to succeed. Necessary processes include the following:

- *Understanding your value relative to competitive offerings and relative to customer needs*

- *Tailoring the offering to the market, customer segment, and/or customer needs*

- *Quantifying your value-in-use in a credible way*

- *Effectively communicating your value to customers*

- *Negotiating the deal, including price/value element tradeoffs*

- *Documenting the value you have delivered (i.e., case studies)*

The systems and tools to support value selling can range from simple, homegrown value calculators (to quantify value at a customer-specific level) to fully integrated value systems. You can use the latter to identify sources of value, quantify the value at a customer-specific level, develop customer-specific professional-level communications and offering packages that facilitate discussion around both value selling and offering/price options as well as document the actual benefits achieved by your customers. If you're serious about imbedding this into the culture and shifting toward world class, consider investing in a holistic system solution. Leverage Point (a spinoff from the Monitor Group) and ZS Associates are examples of companies providing comprehensive value-selling systems that enhance and sustain your value-selling processes.

Without a comprehensive system, you're unlikely to fully make the large gains you desire, sustain the gains, and truly embed value selling into your culture. If it's worth going after, it's worth the investment. Value selling isn't easy, especially if you have a diverse product portfolio or a diverse set of market and customer needs, or you typically sell custom products. If you want your sales force to be effective, you must provide them with the practical, user-friendly tools they need for success. You can't expect your sales force to identify and quantify the customer-specific value for every new deal and create their own customer-tailored value offerings and communication packages unless you give them the tools and systems. Without the tools, don't expect the sales force (and leadership) to persevere on the path.

Some companies that excel at value pricing also modify their sales compensation system to include a behavior element related to value selling. For example, they may compensate sales people based on the number of successful case studies they document or the frequency with which they use value-selling tools.

A Team Positioned to Win!

You're now positioned to win this season. You know how to build a winning team, encourage a supportive environment, set the right pricing strategy, and execute that strategy. You know the processes and systems you'll need to keep winning season after season. It's time to run onto the field and show your fans what you can do. First and ten; do it again . . . and again and again—until your small victories lead up to large victories. *Go team go!*

Acknowledgments

Many people have supported, inspired, or taught me as I have developed my own pricing competency and contributed to the pricing success of the DuPont company.

I owe a debt of gratitude to the courageous leaders who initially persuaded DuPont to create a corporate marketing and sales organization, with a special emphasis on pricing. They provided me the opportunity to be among the key players in leading the pricing and market transformation of DuPont. These leaders included Diane Gulyas, John Hodgson, Mahesh Mansukhani, William White, and David Bills.

I owe a special heartfelt thanks to the key leaders and thought partners on my own pricing team: Todd Freeman, Meena Panchapaksan, and Neil Bunis for their groundbreaking leadership and Harry Christman, Brian Vrabel, and Ed Ziegler for their significant contributions. Many other pricing-resource people contributed significantly to DuPont's success, and I thank them. Also a special thanks to Dan James, Corporate Sales Director, for his partnership and successful efforts at enhancing the sales force competency.

In addition, many DuPont business leaders had the courage and passion to step out and aggressively champion pricing in their businesses. They included Keith Smith, BC Chong, Bill Weber, Rick Olsen, Barry Owens, Peter O'Sullivan, Craig Binetti, Marsha Craig, and Michelle Fite (to name just a few).

Many external firms contributed to my development and success. I particularly acknowledge the consulting firms of: Deloitte, especially Richard Hayes; The Monitor Group (now part of Deloitte), especially Lisa Thompson, Thomas Nagle, and John Hogan; McKinsey Consulting; and the Professional Pricing Society.

Lastly, a number of folks perhaps unknowingly inspired me or influenced my thinking. They include Dick Braun, Parker Hannifin, and Peter Hunt at Pricing Solutions through their insightful presentations to the Professional Pricing Society, Reed Holden of Holden Advisors through his monthly pricing newsletters, Tom Jacobson of Accenture through our thought-provoking discussions, and especially Debbie Weil for both inspiring me and coaching me on the writing of this book.

About the Author

Joanne Smith's passion, purpose, and power lie in managing change within organizations to transform their capabilities for superior results. During her career spanning three decades, she was fortunate to work with enlightened leaders who had the courage to embrace change on a large scale.

Coming in on the creation of DuPont's Corporate Marketing and Sales organization, Joanne became its global marketing and pricing director—the "assistant coach" reporting to the "head coach," or the chief marketing and sales officer. For more than six years, she drove pricing excellence, customer loyalty, and marketing effectiveness at DuPont. As she pulled together the rules and strategies for the pricing game, she was able to "write the playbook" for future teams facing the similar challenges. As DuPont's spokesperson at marketing and pricing conferences, Joanne often explained how the company was able to transform its marketing and pricing for greater financial reward.

Beginning her career at DuPont as a chemical engineer, Joanne first worked in and managed chemical manufacturing plants. For close to 30 years, DuPont tapped into her abilities in a variety of leadership roles, including directing the company's adoption of the rigorous Six Sigma methods for process improvement.

Attaining superior results has always been the "goal line" for this innovative leader and pricing expert. In 2011, Joanne began pioneering an organizational game plan named Commercial Optimization. This ground-breaking approach to finding the sweet spot for profit, capacity, cash, and customer service brought together her expertise in marketing, product-line, demand, and supply-chain management. Today,

Joanne runs Price to Profits, a consulting firm that assists B2B companies in transforming their pricing performance to enhance long-term profitability.

How to contact the author:

Joanne M. Smith

Price to Profits Consulting, LLC
    (http://www.price2profits.com)

info@price2profits.com

Phone 484-459-0166

joanne.m.smith122@gmail.com

Suggested Reading and Resources

Anderson, John C., Nirmalya Kumar, and James A. Narus, *Value Merchants: Demonstrating and Documenting Superior Value in Business Markets*. Boston: Harvard Business School Publishing, 2007.

Baker, Walter, Michael Marn, and Craig Zawanda, *The Price Advantage,* 2nd edition. Wiley Finance, 2010.

Nagle. Thomas T., and John E. Hogan, *The Strategy and Tactics of Pricing: A Guide to Growing More Profitably,* 5th edition. Upper Saddle River, New Jersey: Prentice Hall, 2010.

Professional Pricing Society Conferences and Speakers:

Dick Braun, Vice President Corporate Strategic Pricing, Parker Hannifin, "Building a Pricing Team for All Seasons," May 2010.

Paul Hunt, President Pricing Solutions Ltd. "The Keys to Unlocking Your Organization's Pricing Potential: Creation of a World Class Pricing Organization," April 2007.